RAISING ROBERT

RAISING ROBERT

COPING WITH OUR CHILD'S LIFE THREATENING SYNDROME

JANET FAVORITE

ISBN: 978-0-692-84676-6
Library of Congress Control Number: 2017903617
Printed in the United States of America
First Printing 2017
Cover Design & Interior Book Design: FuzionPrint

Printed by FuzionPrint,
1250 E 115th Street,
Burnsville, MN, 55337 USA

TABLE OF CONTENTS

INTRODUCTION

Twenty-seven years ago I gave birth to Robert, a baby boy with Prader-Willi Syndrome (PWS). PWS is a rare genic disorder caused by a deletion in chromosome 15. It affects about one out of 8,000 to 20,000 people. According to Management of Prader-Willi Syndrome. Although much more is known now, very little information about PWS, and what it meant for my child and family, was available at the time of Robert's birth.

Fast-forward to today, and the IT revolution, especially the internet, has changed everything about the way we access information. This can be a positive or negative thing, depending on the information you access. When researching the syndrome, the information can be dramatic or misleading. I wrote my book to inform people about PWS from a mother's point of view and give insight to what I experienced as the caregiver.

For those who are not familiar with the term "syndrome," it simply means a combination of many symptoms typically occurring together. PWS can often appear to mimic food addiction. People with this syndrome are generally always hungry and always thinking about accessing food. This is because the syndrome removes the brain's "turn-off switch" to food. Normal people feel full when they have eaten a meal because their stomach and brain registers the feeling of fullness and their brain turns off their hunger pains. This doesn't happen for people with PWS. So, just like an addict constantly looking for their next "fix," people with PWS are constantly looking for more food. Their brain never tells them they are full. As a person who dealt with addiction and has been in recovery for over twenty-five years, I understand the aspect of preoccupation and not being able to say no to something. This gives me a unique perspective on the PWS journey.

When Robert was born I had no idea how living with this syndrome would change my life. The fact I operated a small, home-based catering company while raising a child with PWS might seem insane to anyone who knows the syndrome. My life has been challenging, fulfilling, and fun. It is a life I would never have been able to imagine, nor did I have any time to prepare for it. Without the prenatal testing which is available now, we expected Robert to be a "normal" and "healthy" baby until he was born and I was told he had PSW.

Outside of having the opportunity to love and know this amazing son of mine, being a part of the PWS community has meant I've had the opportunity to meet people though work, volunteer opportunities, medical situations, and sports which continue to inspire and amaze me.

However, mine has never been a life of ease. In general, I enjoy being useful and accomplishing a challenge. Raising a child with PWS was a huge challenge, one we could never have handled alone. If you have a child with PWS, your journey will not be the same as mine, because a lot has changed in management of the syndrome in the past several decades. Hopefully my story will help you realize you're not alone. There are many parents out there who understand what you are feeling.

This is the story of how our family managed life with Robert, while accepting help from others. Recently I heard former President Jimmy Carter say God told him, "I have lots of tasks for you to accomplish, don't worry I will send plenty of people to help you." This quote really resonated with me and is truly why I chose to write this book. I want everyone to know help is available for families with a newly diagnosed child, and you are not alone. Organizations that can help you are listed in the back of the book.

My hope is by in writing this book I can give hope to others who are suffering. They may have a child with PWS or another sadness in their lives. I can say to them, "I have been there, I know it's hard." I heard a priest speak recently who said, "You don't have to love your own sad story." I think this is true. I don't have to love the challenges and hurdles I have had to overcome in my life. I do need to find a way to accept them and find happiness wherever I can. This is because I believe God wants us to live a happy life, and we need to strive for it every day.

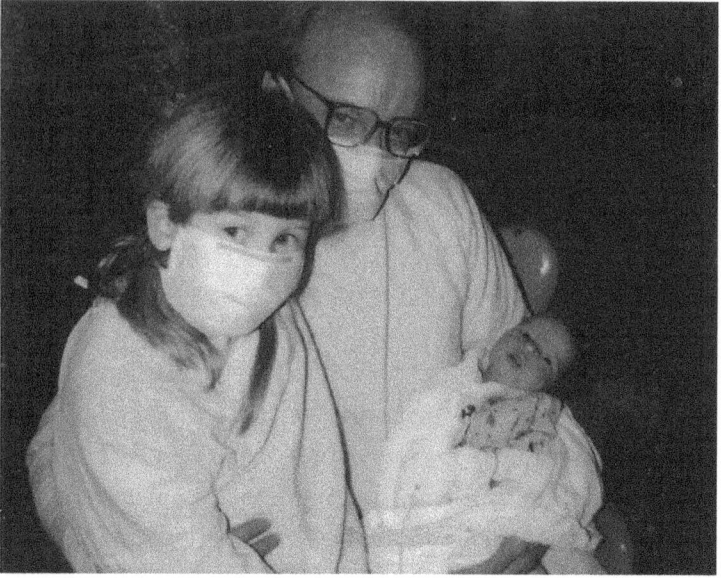

CARA CAREY, AND ROBERT

CHAPTER ONE

THE STORY OF ROBERT'S BIRTH

We silently flinch inwardly when we hear of the death or disfigurement of a child. We say a small prayer, "Thank God that's not my child." We worry about something happening to us or a loved one. One thing I've learned, worrying doesn't change anything. It is said ninety percent of the things we worry about don't come true. I'm not sure is true. A friend's mom used to say, "Worrying is like rocking in a rocking chair, it will wear you out and you'll never get anywhere." I couldn't agree more!

Yet, what if something does happen to us and a tragedy occurs? What if life sends us down a path we would never have chosen? How do you deal with that? And how do you deal with the guilt you feel wondering if could you have done something to prevent it?

My husband and I were so excited about our second child's birth; a birth we had anticipated for nine months. However, the birth itself unfolded in a very different way than we expected. I had survived many unhappy times before Robert's birth. I had already learned life is a combination of good times and bad times. Yet, I was about to learn nothing can prepare you for the emotions you feel when your child suffers.

I was an older mother; thirty-seven at the time of our second child's birth. My husband, Carey, and I had married at age twenty-eight, late for our generation. We wanted a family and were overjoyed several months later when we discovered I was pregnant. Unfortunately, it ended in a miscarriage after three months. We were both grief-stricken, still we were ready to try again. Six months later I was diagnosed with breast cancer. I chose a mastectomy as a treatment option, with reconstruction to follow six months later. It was not an easy time for me or my family. I questioned my doctors about pregnancy. "Could I get pregnant right now?" "If I did get pregnant, would I be able to breast feed?" Of course they reassured me I would be able to have children "down the road" now I needed to focus on recovering and killing the cancer right now. Three months later I was pregnant again. My doctors "freaked" as we used to say. "Don't you know you should have waited five years to get pregnant?" they asked. They were not pleased because some cancers grow with hormonal changes, and I had now put myself, and my unborn child, at high risk for complications and, possibly, secondary cancer.

However, we were fantastically lucky. I gave birth to a healthy baby girl, Cara Lynn. It was the happiest day of my life. So many things had gone wrong for so long. I had felt as though the pregnancy was never going to work, yet, here she was. We had a beautiful baby girl. My body felt full of joy holding our little baby bundle. We named her Cara, love in Italian, and Lynn, my middle name. Although I never breast fed, because the doctors wanted me "back to normal" as quickly as possible to reduce my cancer risk, it didn't matter, I felt so close to her.

Miracles happen. Cara was my personal miracle, well, mine and Carey's. My mom's sobriety was another miracle our whole family shared. I have three siblings, an older brother and two younger sisters. Our mother was an alcoholic from the time I was a teenager. When Cara was born she agreed to treatment. We couldn't wait to have our mom back. We'd grown up with an amazing mom, full of life and happiness. She was for many years, the only family member who drank moderately. I was surrounded in my childhood years with family who either drank or used prescription drugs. Our mother constantly dealt with the chaos created by addicted family members. Our family life deconstructed more and more as I aged. At the end of High School, my parents were divorced, and my mom was drinking heavily. Our brother escaped to the military and I became my teen sisters' parent. Her recovery was like having someone return from the dead. Alcoholism had stolen our mother, now she'd finally returned to us.

My Mom's recovery and Cara inspired me to recover as well. I had also struggled with drug and alcohol dependency issues from a young age. And although I was sober and never used my drug of choice, marijuana, while pregnant, after Cara's birth I started to smoke again while she was napping. However, one day, when Cara was three, right before her nap time, she said to me "Mommy, are you going to smoke your pipe today?" I was shocked. I felt as though I had just been accused of the most heinous crime imaginable. I realized I was doing the same thing my Mom had done. How could I inflict my daughter with the same pain I had felt? I promised myself and my daughter I would get clean immediately. And I did. I stopped using with the help of a group called Women for Sobriety .

The group was similar to AA as they held weekly group meetings. The founder believed genetic difference aside, woman's egos needed building in recovery. Their self-loathing needed to be replaced with positive reinforcement, something AA was slow to acknowledge. Treatment for Women has changed dramatically in the past twenty years. I was ready to be sober and have never used again. The weekly meetings and support from the group helped me achieve the goal of sobriety.

What a relief it was not to think about pot anymore. While talking to my therapist about my struggles with substance abuse, she told me she didn't think I was truly clinically addicted, I have a compulsive personality when it comes to these types of things. Whatever it was, it took over my life. Back when I was using regularly, if someone complimented me, I would think "you wouldn't think I was so great if you knew how much pot I smoke."

Much of my life had been spent thinking about using. When, where, how much, what time, constantly cycled through my brain. I could finally live an honest life, free from drug obsession. And I could be the Mom I always wanted to be for Cara.

Five years passed quickly. I was sober and my cancer remained in remission. Cara grew too fast, as all children do and my husband and I started talking about having a second child. Because of my previous cancer, I visited one of the top female oncologists in the Twin Cities to see if another pregnancy would be safe, or too risky. When I'd had Cara doctors were not able to definitively tell me if I had an estrogen receptive cancer. These types of cancer grow on estrogen, I did not have estrogen receptive cancer the oncologist informed me, which was probably the reason my cancer was not aggressive. I felt very lucky, as not only did this mean I'd survived breast cancer at the age of thirty, it also meant we could move forward to try for another baby. Shortly thereafter I was pregnant again.

During my third pregnancy I was healthy and had no problems. We were excited and couldn't wait to meet our new baby! Well, if I'm being honest, not all of us were excited. Cara wasn't 100 percent sold on the idea of a sister or brother she'd have to share her toys with. What five-year- old child doesn't have those concerns?!

Robert's birth took forty-eight hours. This is not a story I share with new mothers, gleefully telling of the suffering I endured. Day one started at United Hospital in St. Paul at seven am when I checked in as they were going to induce labor. A Pitocin drip was used to kick-start dilation. The day ended at five pm I had had contractions all day, I had not dilated any further. My family practice doctor recommended resting the night and beginning again the next day.

I slept fitfully and wasn't thrilled about starting over again. I stayed strong and centered on when I'd finally get to hold my baby, then it would all be worth it. At two pm the next day, my contractions were out of control and constant, one right after another. The pain was never ending and I finally requested an epidural.

I was still not dilated to ten cm, which meant I was on my way to a "C-section. An OB/GYN specialist was called. Her exam brought good news; I had dilated to five centimeters. She suggested we still try a natural birth. For the next five hours I pushed. The doctor used a vacuum. You could hear the suction cup engage and then disengage with the baby's head. I had people pressing on my stomach, helping me push with each contraction, yet the baby would not come. Finally, after what felt like forever, an emergency C-section was performed and Robert was born.

I don't remember seeing the baby. My only memories are of being in severe pain. I couldn't even turn and reach my nurse call button because it hurt too much. The nurses were wonderful and placed warmed blankets over me and gave me pain medication. It felt so comforting. I thought my ordeal was finally over.

The next morning, I met my baby boy. He had a huge bruise on his head, otherwise perfect in every other way. Carey and I named him Robert, and we were thrilled. We had our beautiful six-year-old daughter, Cara, and now we had a beautiful baby boy. We even had our dog, Sasha, at home. We were the "perfect" All-American family, or so we thought.

Later in the day, Carey and I were told Robert was unable to suck on the bottle, he would have to go to the neonatal intensive care unit (NICU). Terror and fear doesn't begin to describe what Carey and I felt. How could this have happened? He was perfect this morning, and we couldn't understand what had caused the change. All my prenatal tests were fine, Yes, I was an older mother at thirty-seven, but I had had a successful pregnancy with Cara, so no problems had been expected. We felt like the bottom dropped out beneath us. A note to parents who may currently be pregnant or considering it in the future, screening tests have vastly improved since I had Robert in the late eighties. Today, many chromosomal syndromes and other health concerns can be identified during pregnancy that weren't possible to detect when I was pregnant.

My sister, Catherine (Cath), had planned a birthday party for Robert in the hospital. Since she had been watching Cara for us, she thought it would be a fun and special way to introduce Cara to her brand new brother. Cath also brought her daughter Kelly, also six, and only weeks younger than Cara, and her son, Steven, who was nine. The kids were excited as they carried Robert's very first birthday cake to the maternity unit. Of course this was before cell phones and social media were ubiquitous, so Cath had no idea while she and the kids were pulling together the party, we were trying to cope and understand what was going to become of our precious baby boy.

As Cath and the kids finally made it to the hospital floor, she stopped at the nurse's station before entering the room to make sure she had the right room. The charge nurse abruptly told her, "The baby is no longer here. He is in the Neonatal Intensive Care Unit. I can't give you any more information." Cath, who is a nurse herself, understood the implications from the clinical side immediately. Having never been in this situation before, as a family member of a patient, she immediately felt upset and furious at the nurse's lack of empathy. She made a valiant attempt to cover her emotions from the kids and us as they all entered my room, her stricken face revealed her fear and concern. Quietly she said to me, "Jan, what is wrong with the baby?" I could only tell her what we knew, "Robert isn't able to eat. He is too weak to suck." We had no idea a two week stay in the NICU was in Robert's future. For the rest of the evening, we both struggled to keep things together, enjoying the birthday cake and trying not to frighten the children.

My sister's medical background in nursing made her insist on immediate answers. There were none. Although as Robert grew up, we would learn much and get many answers, Cath's role was already set, she would spend the rest of Robert's life being both Auntie, and nurse. She would assess, and reassess, and tell us the truth as she saw it.

Our baby had no diagnosis, only hypertonia, a state of low muscle tone which results in reduced muscle strength, commonly known as floppy baby syndrome. Robert was a floppy baby. He didn't suckle and he had a huge bruise on his forehead from all the contractions he had endured, and he never cried. Our neurologist, Dr. G, was a kind man, yet he had no answers to our questions either. Multiple tests were done during Robert's two week NICU stay. Each day we would arrive at the NICU hoping "this would be the day they'd find out what was wrong, and fix it." It never arrived.

Years later I talked to other women who had given birth to children with hypertonia. Their birth stories were often very similar to mine. A gynecologist told me after Robert's birth "Babies need to actively participate in the birthing process. If they have low muscle tone, their participation is limited and complications can arise." After my experience, what she said made perfect sense.

If you've never been inside an NICU before, count yourself lucky. For every parent and loved one who has spent time in an NICU, I want you to know I understand. For Carey and me, walking into the NICU at United Hospital meant seeing twelve babies in twelve tiny incubators, with electrodes and tubing attached to their tiny little bodies. Some babies only weighed a pound or two. These babies had been born too soon and had multiple problems. Robert was a full-term baby and he looked enormous and healthy in comparison. The nurses were so supportive and reassuring. Any parent who has lived through an NICU experience knows it's the incredible nurses that get you through the day. We experienced support and care, for our baby and the whole family. Throughout the two weeks of his hospitalization, all of the testing was inconclusive. Although PWS was first discovered in 1956, it is rare, and resources for diagnosis were not readily available at the time. All the doctors could tell us was other than the hypertonia (low muscle tone), and inability to suck, Robert was alert, beautiful, and responsive. So, after fourteen long days, plans were made for his discharge.

The hospital required we learn to gavage feed before leaving. This is done by inserting a tube down the baby's throat and slowly pouring the formula down it. It went well; I was able to get the tube down with my second attempt. Optimistically, I was sure once Robert came home, we would not actually have to use this technique. We were thrilled, yet fearful, to finally bring our baby home. I remember being annoyed with our nurse the day he was discharged. All I wanted to do was take Robert home, she insisted we feed him before leaving. I look back now and understand she was not only simply doing her job, and was also continuing the amazing care we had consistently received. However, at the time I just wanted to be out of there. I recognized a deep conviction of what best for Robert. This was going to be a feeling I became very familiar with throughout the years and would carry me though many years of both heartbreak and joy.

Looking at the bigger picture now, I can see we were fortunate to have had so many things in our lives to be grateful for. Yes, our son's health was questionable, but our health insurance had covered everything, our family was supportive and loving, our six-year-old daughter was beautiful and bright, and we had our own home and many supportive friends. With so many blessings, we would find the strength to meet every challenge Robert's health would bring us.

As we left the hospital, our doctors and nurses were reassuring. One nurse in particular told me, "He's going to be fine." I'm not sure she realized how important her words were to me. Several years later, I had the opportunity to tell her when we reconnected at our church how her words of reassurance, had gotten me though some very rough times.

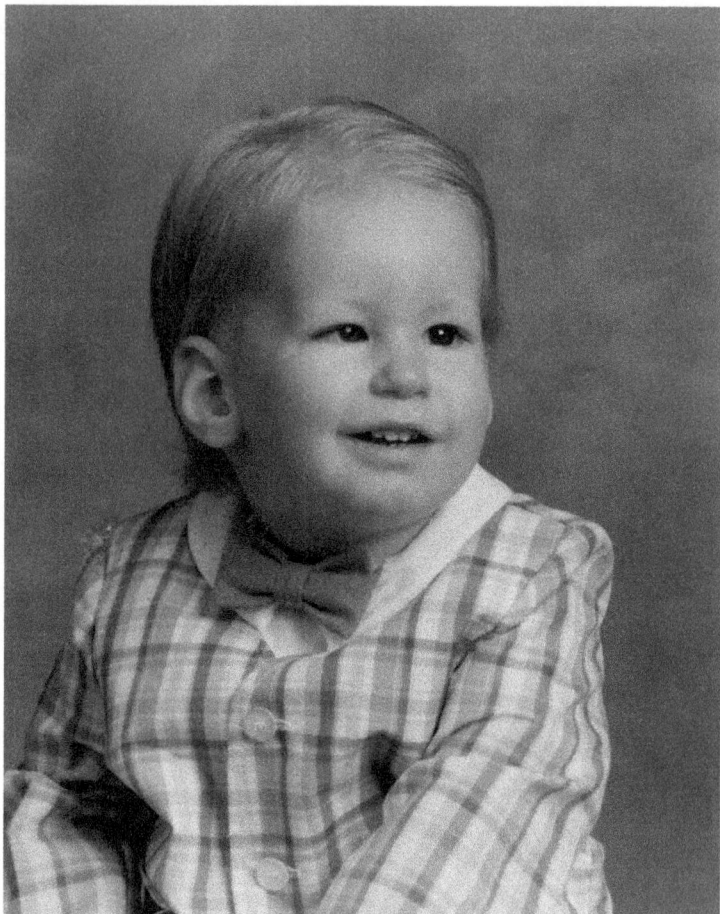

ROBERT 1990

CHAPTER TWO

YOU WORK, I'LL DO THE CAREGIVING

Carey had always been the breadwinner of the family. His work had supported the family after Cara was born, so it continued. Like many "stay at home" moms, I had done part-time work over the years, including: daycare, waitressing, and even as an independent caterer. After Robert's birth, Carey and I had an unspoken agreement, I would handle all of Robert's medical needs and he would work. I suppose many would say we had a traditional marriage, or at least, what had been traditional, in my experience.

Robert needed several follow-up appointments after leaving the hospital. Carey had never been comfortable in medical environments. Instead it stressed him out and made him extremely uncomfortable, which would then be expressed as impatience or anger towards the doctors, me or anyone near us. Honestly, it was easier for everyone and kept our life stable for me to take Robert to his appointments and for Carey to remain the breadwinner.

It would be the pattern of life for our family. While researching this book, I interviewed other women with special needs children. Many of them have similar stories of becoming their child's main caregiver, often giving up fulltime employment to focus on the medical needs including frequent doctor and clinic visits, physical and occupational therapy, and other specialty appointments. Throughout the book I will share some of the amazing stories of women I've met along the way.

Ashely's story

Ashely gave birth to baby Micah almost two years ago, roughly twenty-five years after I had Robert. Ashley's labor didn't progress normally and she ultimately needed to have a cesarean section as Micah got stuck and was unable to move down the birth canal. Once born, Micah was diagnosed almost immediately with Prader-Willi Syndrome. The health system also provided a pediatric geneticist who informed Ashley and her husband about the syndrome and what they could expect. They were, of course, devastated upon hearing how severely the syndrome could affect their child. Both parents have strong faith which they leaned on throughout this difficult time.

Once they processed the initial diagnosis, Ashley and her husband realized they have a great support system in their family, friends, and their church. Ashely's sister said "I will support you in whatever you need, even if you need to move next door to me." Having this support around them would be, and will continue to be, a huge resource for Ashley, her husband and Micah.

One of the aspects of PWS is small stature and small features. With the success and advent of biotechnology, growth hormones have become an active treatment for this aspect of PWS. Micah thus started growth hormones at three months of age. Like many PWS children, doctor and physical therapy appointments began to consistently take several days out of each calendar month. Ashley feels blessed, she is able to be a stay-at-home mom, as she can't imagine juggling her son's needs with a full-time job. She is also thankful for the specialists who are part of Micah's care team, many of whom she found through contacts at the PWS Association of Minnesota. "Their doctors have been amazing," she says.

Ashley told me "There are many days I cry, then I think of all the other suffering children I see with cancer or other illnesses." She wants to help her son succeed, and she focuses on that when she is having a hard time coping with her own stress.

CARA AND ROBERT

CHAPTER THREE

SPENDING A LOT OF TIME WITH HEALTHCARE PROFESSIONALS

I felt comfortable at the clinic in Children's Hospital in St Paul from the start. My mother had actually worked there for several years, which gave me an insiders' view, because she could give me suggestions and insights about many of the doctors who worked there.

My mom supported us though many worrisome appointments. She became someone I depended on greatly. Just being with her calmed me down. She was very giving and I know she supported my sisters as well. Our mother never said "no" to any last minute requests for help.

Mom once told me she knew I was "selfish enough" to handle taking care of Robert. The words may sound harsh. Considering her caretaking background they were accurate. Many caregivers get lost in the disease, syndrome or illness of the person they are supporting. Often finding they no longer have an identity outside of their role as caretaker. And although Robert was one of my biggest priorities, she knew I would continue to enjoy my own life, as I had in the past. I had survived breast cancer at thirty-one, and addiction. I knew how precious life was. Just like with mothering "normal" children, it is crucial to have some time to yourself and do things you enjoy. My mom recognized it made you a better mom, a better caregiver and a better person if you had time to recharge your own batteries. For me it meant spending time with friends, the people who made me laugh. Our imperfect families, husbands, and own flawed selves gave us lots of topics to discuss.

During Robert's first months of life, denial and I would become good friends. Of course, as a mother, you will do everything for your child. As I predicted, the gavage technique we had learned in the hospital proved unnecessary. Our baby learned to suck, and would eat three ounces at a time. It was time consuming, still it felt like a victory. The doctors continued testing nothing appeared conclusive. We still didn't know what was going on with Robert. Both Carey and I hoped and prayed at some point this would all be over. Robert would get over his traumatic birth and be normal.

At three months, our neurologist suggested a chromosome test. He mentioned Prader-Willi, a syndrome with a chromosome deletion. We didn't really understand anything about PWS, in fact, we'd never even heard of it. However, the test result proved inconclusive, and we were back at square one with no answers. It was the only test available, so we didn't have any other option in finding a diagnosis.

In the meantime, the doctor recommended early childhood intervention. This meant meeting regularly with a physical therapist and a speech therapist to work on large and small muscle skills.

The language of early childhood specialists can be reassuring. They speak of "delays" and you figure, "Okay, at some point our child will catch up." We worked as a team to help Robert improve, the first years of our son's life consisted of milestones consistently unmet.

Because Robert's speech was delayed, we taught him sign language to allow us to better communicate with him and to try and stimulate speech. The tongue is one big muscle, and it took a lot of therapy for him to master speech. Once he did, he became very inquisitive little motor mouth, which everyone around him loved. Robert was always talking to people and they loved it. Looking back, I can see why; he was a very happy child, fair haired and adorable in his tiny blue glasses and perpetually sunny smile.

We also patched one eye to encourage the other to work harder and develop muscle strength. People would stop me at the grocery store, "Why is your boy wearing a patch?" they would ask. I'd think "Why do you care, it's none of your business." Most of the time I would say, "Oh, he has a lazy eye; we are trying to avoid surgery." Nowadays eye patches and other similar therapy tools seem to be more prevalent so perhaps mothers currently don't encounter as many questioning glares, when Robert was little it wasn't common to see children with a patch on their eye.

Robert would have surgery for his lazy eye at age three by ophthalmologist, Dr. Richard Stanek, who worked at St Paul Eye Clinic. Dr. Stanek is a kind and reassuring surgeon, who did a wonderful job correcting Robert's eye problem.

Several years later, my friend and catering client, Sandy, and I were discussing Robert's surgery. Sandy spends much of her life advocating for special needs people. She was looking for a surgeon to operate on a woman who had almost none of one pupil showing. I said, "Oh I wish she could have Dr. Stanek do the surgery, he did such a great job on Robert." "Do you think he would do the surgery for free?" Sandy asked. When I told her I didn't know, she replied, "Why don't you ask him." I agreed to talk with him, internally I thought, yikes, what have I gotten myself into?

Dr. Stanek agreed immediately when I asked him to donate his services. The surgery was a success in many ways. It taught me to ask for what I needed. People can always say no. I also was able meet the young women who had eye surgery. I stared into her two beautiful bright blue eyes as I shook her hand. "I helped make this possible" I thought. It made me want to do more.

Normally, babyhood goes by so fast. In the blink of an eye, your baby is rolling over, sitting up, crawling. And then boom, he's a toddler, starting to walk and talk all over the place. Robert was my perpetual baby. At the age of three he was still not walking. We carried him around and continued to care for him much like any six-month old who is sitting up and scooting around and not really mobile. One big difference was Robert had the intelligence and verbal ability of a three-year-old. However, his speech was hard for people to understand due to his muscle tone, he often needed me, Cara, or my niece Kelly as an interpreter. I would make off-hand jokes sometimes about being given the gift of an "ever-baby" when my stress and emotions got away from me. I held most of my emotions inside, a ball of fear permanently residing in my lower stomach. I did my best to ignore it and instead focus on the progress Robert had made, no one's perfect, right?

Our biggest fear was wondering if Robert would ever walk. No one could answer. The toys people gave him did not interest him. His favorite pastime was lying on the floor, holding a piece of string above his head. String seemed to hold a "doorway" to his imagination and he spent a lot of time in his imaginary world. String continued to fascinate him and function as a security blanket of sorts for many years.

My sister and I often took all of our children swimming. We would work together, to encourage Robert to move in the water. Finally, by age three he was starting to be able to walk in the shallow end of the pool. This gave us so much hope for a future when he could hold his weight without the buoyancy of the water.

On the Christmas Eve shortly before he turned four, Robert took three steps. We were at my older brother Tom's home, as we always were on Christmas Eve. His Uncle Tom caught and hugged him tight, tears rolling down his cheeks. We couldn't believe it! Our family deemed it a joyful Christmas miracle. Robert was also speaking more by then, however, Cara and Kelly would continue to need to interpret his imperfect speech to others, particularly the grownups, and even Carey and me, from time-to-time.

My sister Cath started nursing school about this time. I helped take care of her children while she went to school and worked. Our nephew, Steven, was three years older than Cara and Kelly, who were only six weeks apart. The two girls were like siblings, totally opposite in every way. Each of them wanted what the other had, and was willing to fight to get it.

Kelly was loving, patient, and kind to her younger cousin, Robert. She often stayed inside with him while the older cousins played outdoors. Her severe asthma had made her susceptible to every cough and cold, so from a very young age she spent more time indoors where the environment was controlled. Kelly shared her love of reading and singing with Robert. In later years, she would read almost the entire Harry Potter series out loud to him, with the exception of the last two books, which Robert was able to read on his own and then discuss with her. Kelly memorized and performed every Disney movie song.

Robert's audience of one, watched in amazement, mesmerized by her actions.

COUSIN KELLY AND ROBERT

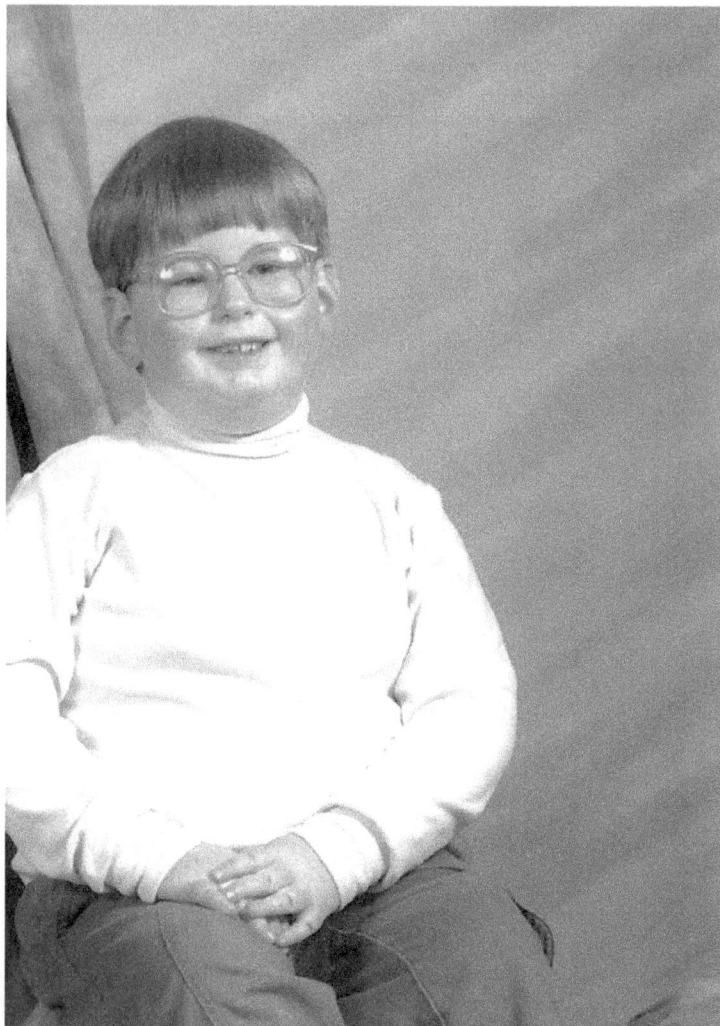

BEGINNING OF WEIGHT GAIN

CHAPTER FOUR

FAILURE TO THRIVE SHIFTS TO MASSIVE WEIGHT GAIN

After the first few years, we were grateful because so many things were going right. "Maybe he will catch up," we thought. Robert was such a darling baby and toddler. He had a sunny disposition and he never cried. You could cuddle with him as long you liked, and he would never fuss to get out of your arms. My perpetual baby wouldn't last forever,

Abruptly at age three, Robert started gaining weight at an alarming rate. We were baffled, he ate so slowly, how could this be? After visiting our family practice doctor who couldn't explain what was happening, we went back to Children's Hospital to see specialists. This time it was suggested we see an endocrinologist, Dr. X., who was well respected in the medical community. He did a thorough exam, and took measurements of every part of Robert's anatomy. He suggested limiting juice and calories, "Come back in three months' time," he said. With no real answers why this was happening, we did as the doctor suggested in hope of some change, yet Robert's weight continued to increase.

On our follow-up visit three months later, Dr. X. said "I think Robert has Prader- Willi. This is the reason for the weight gain." "No," I said, "he was already tested as an infant and it was inconclusive."

Instead of pushing back, Dr. X. left the room, only to return with two sheets of paper. They were copies of two pages from a medical textbook showing naked eight-year-old boys, all very short and obese. "This is what your son has," he stated. "See how he has all the same features: small hands and feet, almond eyes, short stature, and heavy set." He offered no words of advice or comfort, it wasn't his style. He was a straight-to-the-point, no frills, kind of doctor. This wasn't easy for me, although I did get used to it over the years. I was so outraged I momentarily pictured myself ripping up the papers in his face as he handed them to me. Instead, what I actually did was tell him, "I don't agree; the tests he had were inconclusive." I then promptly dressed my baby and left.

I left the hospital scared, disheartened, and angry. "This was supposed to be a children's hospital. How could he have given me this information with no compassion? Doesn't he understand the diagnosis has a huge impact? The doctor showed no consideration for how his words would affect us. What a jerk! How would we manage PWS? I'm sure he's wrong," I told myself. I was too overwhelmed to even consider Dr. X. might be right, and I would continue to deny he had been right for many years. The future he forecast was just too grim.

During the early nineties, Robert's infancy and toddler years, the first days of medical information on the internet were just starting. Carey worked with computers and, as such, we had had computers and internet much sooner than most households. Carey immediately began to do research and found people with PWS generally only live to be forty years old. They then typically die of morbid obesity. It also stated PWS children are generally "angels" as infants and toddlers. Incredibly docile and even tempered, many never fuss or cry, at age five or so their personalities change. The children begin to be subject to uncontrollable rages and hunger. Although Robert certainly fit the "angel child" criteria I was certain I did not see a personality change in my son. I continued to tell myself "No! No! No! Dr. X. is wrong!"

Even with the information Carey found on the internet, general information was not readily available. I did find a national support group for PWS people and their families. Fortunately, they had a local chapter in Minnesota. Although I wasn't ready to accept Robert having PWS, I was hoping I could find out more about it. When I reached out, I was connected with the father of an older boy, about seventeen, who had PWS. His son was in crisis and they could no longer care for him at home and were placing him in a group home. At this point in my life a group home was a completely foreign concept. I would cry when I thought of Cara, then ten, leaving home and attending college. I couldn't even imagine what a group home was and why I would ever consider putting my child in one. I was convinced my darling boy would never be put in such a place.

When I look back I'll never know why this father shared such an alarming story with a mother he didn't know, and who was just trying to understand PWS. He must have been preoccupied and anxious. At the time, all it did was convince me not to contact this support group again. I had attended several support groups in the past for both my breast cancer and addiction and found them helpful yet they can also be unsettling. You can hear sad stories of unhappy transitions or deaths. Several women in my cancer support group died. Their deaths were frightening and I used to wonder, what if it happened to me? So, when I had such a negative initial experience with the PWS group, I became unwilling to open myself to more negative information. Now, I'll never know if a support group would have helped us during those early days of diagnosis.

Kristy's Story

Kristy Rickenbach, who, at the time of writing this book, is the president of the Minnesota chapter of the Prader-Willi Association, had a similar experience. She listened to the father of a child with PWS say, "Our children will grow up to be monsters!" She was also told by a doctor, "her child had one of the gravest syndromes imaginable." Instead of backing away from conflict, Kristy decided she never wanted to hear of another parent being told these things. She became determined to make a difference. She is now President of PWS Minnesota.

Through her work and the hard work of countless others, the PWS Association now offers newly diagnosed families many resources, including a Package of Hope, which gives reliable information to caregivers about what they can expect, as well as offering them a mentoring program. This is available through PWSA USA.

By the time Robert was four, we realized instead of catching up to his peers like we hoped, he clearly had a problem. It would impact our lives indefinitely. I developed a pattern of addressing only what I could manage at the time. I think this may happen to many people when they face a crisis. You can only process what you can process. I was able to handle situations as they occurred. I was only able to focus only on short-term goals in order to cope with the unknown aspects of Robert's physical and mental state.

A mother's life is so busy. You juggle work, laundry, meals, play time at the park, walking the dog, activities, etc. The list goes on and on. You do this all the while trying to sustain your marriage or partnership. With normal stress, most marriages have a fifty-fifty chance of success, you add the additional stress of having a special needs child, and it's no surprise parents of these children have only a twenty percent relationship survival rate.

My marriage certainly felt the strain. Throughout Robert's childhood Carey and I both grieved the loss of a "perfect child." The son who would grow up, attend college, get married, have his own children and life, did not exist for us. Its absence created pain and stress between

Carey and me because the grief was too painful to discuss. In order to cope and support each other, we simply tried to live one day at a time. For us, it made a difficult situation bearable.

Many would be quick to judge our coping mechanism declaring it unhealthy to shield yourself through denial. We were not alone; I saw other young parents of special needs children also coping by denying problems. You can only address what you acknowledge. Our physical therapist told me about a special education teacher, who was a parent of a five-year-old child who had special needs the mother did not recognize. I was initially surprised because this person had a master's degree in special education. As I reflected, I realized everyone uses denial to protect themselves from what they do not want to know and are not ready to handle. It is not always a bad thing. It's a human coping mechanism helping all of us survive. And sometimes you need it. You just hope denial doesn't keep a child from getting the help they need.

Chapter Five

Finding Gillette

After my horrible experience with Dr. X., I made up my mind never to go back. I reached out for referrals and several places were suggested for Robert's care. Someone mentioned Gillette Children's Hospital, a specialty hospital focusing on special needs children. When I looked into it, I found out they even had a clinic specifically for Prader-Willi children. Even though I was still certain Robert didn't have PWS, I was sure if I brought him in, we would receive another diagnosis and finally get some real answers. One call later and we had an appointment.

Gillette did so many things the right way. I'd never had such a positive experience with my own care, Cara's or with Robert's many needs. It immediately assured us we'd found a place for answers. When we got there and checked-in, instead of spending a long time in one waiting room or another, they immediately recorded Robert's height and weight, and took blood samples for the endocrinologist. I found out this was their standard practice, no matter if your doctor needed x-rays, tests, etc. This approach was great as it lessened my anxiety and Robert's, making us more comfortable about having to be at the doctor's yet again.

We were scheduled to see Dr. Michael Ainslie, another endocrinologist. He was a big man, over six feet tall. And throughout our appointment, he looked at Robert and me while speaking. He also had a soft, reassuring voice and he included Robert in the conversation. Perhaps it was his young age or his needs, I hadn't had a doctor treat Robert as anything more than the "patient'. Dr. Ainslie treated Robert as a person with just as much voice about his treatment and life, as himself or me. I have never met another specialist who was so compassionate, respectful, and kind. I would learn compassion, respect and kindness was inherent in everyone who worked at Gillette, including Dr. Ainslie's nurse, Carolyn Jones.

However, the appointment did not give me the good news I had hoped for. Dr. Ainslie said, "Robert does not have a definitive diagnosis of Prader-Willi, he does have many of the same problems associated with it. Let's try to help with those problems." What a wise man he was. He gave me the information in a kind and indirect way and focused instead on how we could improve Robert's health. And really, what difference did it make what you called it, as long as he knew how to help Robert. Looking back though, it wouldn't surprise me if Robert's chart listed PWS from the start.

We went to the clinic every three months to see Dr. Ainslie, along with any support staff he felt would help. A nutritionist and phycologist would see us in the same room, on the same day, minutes apart. If you've ever had to take a child to multiple appointments, you know how wonderful this system was. This was the "Gillette way'. Instead of running around like a crazy person trying to get

Robert from room to room, building to building, to make every appointment, the specialists came to us. All we had to do was go to the hospital and stay in our patient room. The world would be a better place if all clinical operations were this considerate of their patients' needs.

Because Gillette was a specialty hospital for children with special needs, we saw many severely compromised children at each visit. It broke my heart to see how they struggled. I spoke of my feelings to a staff person one day, "I wonder how some of these parents make it through the day with the challenges they have to face?" She looked at me and answered, "I wonder who those parents are? I've talked to so many parents and they all wonder how the "other parents cope." This astonished me, as some children were so severely disabled, I wasn't sure I would handle their needs if they were mine. Then I realized Robert was also disabled and someone may see him and feel that way about my child. As his mother, living with Robert's issues had become my normal. I guess it must be true for the other mothers as well.

The Hospital was a place of support and reassurance. I felt I could get the information I needed there. Dr. Ainslie and Nurse Jones were trustworthy and capable. The information they gave me was for the here and now, Robert's future was not discussed. Maybe they understood how I coped, or, maybe Robert's progress was just too unclear to determine future goals. I may never truly know.

I came to dread certain parts of each three-month visit. The most difficult moment occurred at check-in when I would have concrete proof I could not deny of how much weight Robert had gained and how little he had grown.

Friends and relatives had a hard time understanding how easily Robert gained weight. Cookies and candy were rewards other children were given with little or no thought. It was so hard to say no to someone offering Robert a small treat and making him feel left out. I remember discussing this with our pastor's wife. I know she was at a loss for how to give me advice, instead she jokingly said, "Maybe you should put a sign on Robert saying, "Please Don't Feed the Monkeys." I thought this was hilarious, and it felt good to laugh about it.

Laughing got me though many rough days. I had the choice of laughing or crying, and laughing was always my preferred mode of coping. Maybe it's because my mom had always made people laugh. I remember when I was ten watching her with her friends and wanting to be like that. She would occasionally host a practice, for the singing group she belonged to, and the women often broke into laughter at her clever asides. I hoped to be like her when I grew up. As it turns out, I don't think I've ever been as funny as my mom. I do have an ability to make light of difficult situations, something with which I've had a lot of practice over the years.

One of my mom's friends had a daughter my age who attended the same high school as I did, Highland Park in

St Paul. We stayed connected following high school. In those early years we would sit at the counter of the Bridgeman's Ice Cream parlor in Dinky Town Minneapolis, laughing about the crazy situations and predicaments in which we found ourselves. We used to joke we should hire ourselves out to comedy clubs.

My high school friend and I were also a part of a larger group of friends—there were seven of us in total. We called ourselves the Kathy O gang, named after my friend Kathy. There was no better group in the world to get you laughing about your life. Our serious topics always ended up with someone making a goofy comment the group found hilarious. They've always been the people I lean on and who lean on me throughout my life, especially when I had a particularly hard day with Robert and just needed a moment to smile, laugh and remember the lighter side of life.

ROBERT RIDING HIS BIKE

CHAPTER SIX

EVERYTHING CAN BE THERAPY

By now, normal certainly didn't describe our household. Some of the things which continued to surprise me were the things only special needs parents and families understand. For example, we used the local park for physical therapy. Going to the park wasn't just about fun and getting the kids tired, it was about growing muscle strength. Robert was encouraged to climb up slides, instead of sliding down. This would strengthen his legs and core. Sometimes as we maneuvered Robert up the slide, you could feel others watching and wondering, "what's wrong with that kid?" I know my Cara felt this keenly, and it was very hard for her at times. What little girl wants to be stared at because her little brother is different?

We also used grocery store parking lots for exercise, moving slowly to a store's entrance. One day we had to pass three tough-looking teenagers who were sitting on a car bumper smoking. I always felt vulnerable moving so slowly, I worked hard not to let it show, or to hurry Robert in any way. "Hi," my Robert said to those boys with a big smile. "Hi little man," they responded, smiling back. This small event transformed my thinking about how I thought about others. I tried, from that moment on, not to prejudge people simply by their appearance. Instead, I try to treat each person equally. Try of course is the key word, I'm not always successful.

Sandy's Story

I met Sandy Klas at one of the first small dinner parties I catered. She looked me in the eyes as I told my story about having a disabled child. I knew right away she "got it." So many people look uncomfortable, or can't meet your eyes when you talk about special needs. It was clear she understood my terror of sailing into unchartered waters. Sandy would become my client, then my friend, and finally my mentor.

Sandy, it turned out, is the mother of two special needs children and four "normal" children. She is a generation older than I, when families were generally larger. She has great insight into the feelings of the siblings of special needs children in general, and Cara, in particular. One day she told me, "With today's smaller families the siblings of special needs children will have no one to share the care of a special needs sibling. When the parents are gone one sibling will have total responsibility." She realized the sole burden Cara, and so many like her, were already dealing with, and what Cara will have on her shoulders as she ages, and we are no longer there to care for Robert.

Our daughter lost the mother she had for her first six years when Robert was born. I came home from the hospital with him, scared and preoccupied. Sandy told me it was similar for her, with many more siblings, she'd said to her other children "There is one of me and six of you, deal with it." With six children, even if none of them had special needs, individually, they would have had little time alone with their mom, but, they had each other. It's not fair to your "normal" children your neediest child gets more attention, that's just the way it is. As such, siblings of special needs children often are not loving caregivers.

Sandy and her family own a company called TAPE MARK and have devoted many hours of community service to help people with disabilities. They host a golf tournament every June in South St. Paul for Arc of Minnesota. Sandy's energy and enthusiasm for raising money for causes she believes in never ceases to amaze me.

Because Cara was already six when Robert came along, she had years of being our only child and my primary focus. She resented Robert, and it isn't surprising she did. She told me one day she was pinching her brother while he lay in his crib. "Move!" she would shout at him. When siblings are older when the new baby comes along, they often act out since any attention is better than none. We certainly saw this in our daughter.

I tried everything I heard of to help Cara cope. Even at her young age, I noticed Cara was gaining weight. Maybe this was due to her fear, anger, or depression over her brother, or maybe it was because I wasn't as aware of her eating habits. All I knew was I wanted her to be healthy. I found a program offering a family approach to overeating. It incorporated healthy eating, exercise, and journaling. I thought it might not only help Cara, maybe it could help me with managing Robert's continual weight gain as well. However, after attending the program and asking Cara about it, hoping she'd enjoyed it, she said, "I didn't feel fat until you made me go to a Fat Program!"

We also tried a siblings of special needs children support group, put on by ARC of Minnesota. ARC is concerned with the total life of the individual, including their siblings. "One of the girls in the group was raped by an older brother's friend," my daughter remarked after a session. Cara used shock as a tool to get my attention and also to get back at me. It was her coping mechanism and a way to channel her anger. As usual, I did not disappoint her with my reaction. "What? What did the person leading the group have to say about that?" I asked. The shock I felt was exposed in my voice. "Oh nothing much," she answered simply. I was her best audience. I'm sure, looking back, like any support group leader is taught, if a girl did make a statement like that, they would have handled it appropriately and helped her get services if needed. Cara's remark was about getting a response out of me, nothing more. We would attend other meetings but it seemed futile. Cara did not like to share, and she didn't want to be involved in any of these types of activities.

We moved to the suburbs when Cara was in fifth grade. Gunfire was heard across the street from the Montessori school she attended in St Paul, and for the rest of the year, the children were being taught to drop and roll. Our realtor laughed with us about white flight. It was the best decision for our family. Montessori had not been a good fit for Cara.

Kelly and Steven attended this school, did well, and would finish elementary school there, Cara was only reading at a third grade level in fifth grade.

In her new elementary school, which used a more traditional approach to teaching, her new teacher thought ADD might be part of Cara's problem. Many girls actually go undiagnosed because they are not generally as hyperactive as ADD boys. She encouraged us to have her tested, which we did. After extensive testing she was diagnosed with ADD. This was a blessing for us, because with the diagnosis, Cara was given extra help in school and was soon doing better.

ADD also explained many of Cara's characteristics and personality traits. The more I learned the more I thought "Carey is exactly like that!" Father and daughter were so alike. Both would start projects and then quickly lose interest; they had amazing intellect both had struggled with school; Carey's office looked as though someone had ransacked the place and Cara's room was beyond messy. As a result, Carey was diagnosed with ADD himself shortly after Cara.

Our family doctor put both Carey and Cara on medication. My husband loved it, while my daughter said she never felt like herself on it.

We were also destined to spend many hours in therapy. Cara would shrug in response to a therapist's probing questions. Both were able to disengage from uncomfortable feelings; they didn't want to talk about emotions. Instead they tried to ignore their feelings which often resulted in their emotions and stress coming out as anger in other situations.

I desperately felt if I could only phrase what I had to say in the right way, I would be able to help Cara. Of course, I realize now this was just wishful thinking and doesn't ever work. Memories of our verbal encounters still pain me. She would lie on her bed while I preached at her from the doorway. Her lack of attention was clearly apparent, somehow I couldn't stop talking. Even if my internal voice was saying, "Shut up Jan!" I couldn't stop myself, and it only pushed her further away. After lamenting about the situation between Cara and me to a friend one day, she said, "You can't put old heads on young bodies." And she is right, Cara didn't want to hear what I had to say, she was going to have to make her own mistakes. My speeches to her and others helped no one, they only fed my habitual preoccupation with needing to fix things. After many years of this futile cycle, I changed tactics and learned singing, aloud or in my head, helped me stop the fruitless process of creating and delivering the perfect bit of advice. Shockingly, many people are still able to live their lives without my help.

WE CAN RIDE

ROBERT AT SPECIAL OLYMPIC HORSE SHOW

CHAPTER SEVEN

HOW HORSE THERAPY AND CAMP COURAGE GAVE ME HOPE

As the years went on, Carey continued to seek information through the internet. And as the internet grew, more and more resources became available to him. Carey learned typically at age five children with PWS change. Often, they are angel children, then behavior problems start to occur, including regular tantrums. I would lie awake night after night, after learning of this, afraid of this happening. When Robert turned five and we didn't see a major change occur during the year, I felt such relief. "I'm sure this means he doesn't really have PWS," I reassuringly told myself.

Hindsight as they say is twenty-twenty, and looking back I know it's true. Robert's behaviors began to emerge so gradually they initially went unnoticed. We slowly began to have problems with food and food related rituals. A lot of children have favorite foods, or get into a routine of what they like to eat for a meal. Robert began eating exactly the same breakfast every day, and if the breakfast ritual deviated in any way, he would cry inconsolably. He was also unable to share any food, not even a single French fry. If, for example, I realized he had too much on his plate or someone unknowingly grabbed something from him, he would cry and stubbornly become fixated on getting back whatever was taken away. We tried to avoid this by ensuring he had exact portions on his plate before he ever saw it and keeping others from sharing with him.

There was a six-year age difference between my children so sharing toys had never been an issue. We began to notice his behavior change when other children visited. He would not share his toys or books and he adamantly refused to allow others to use his things. People do not understand this is also part of his disability. When he was young it was really hard to explain why I wasn't punishing him for not sharing, when sharing is an important part of learning how to get along with others.

Although Robert had many toys, his only play involved his string—which was an imaginative escape for him, and sorting the colored pieces from a Lite Bright toy. He would sort the colored pieces he called pegs over and over again into groups. He never actually used the Lite Bright in the traditional way, it was merely a container for his pegs. He only sorted the pegs and left them exactly how he wanted them, wherever he wanted them. Of course, we couldn't have pegs lying around and he wasn't able to clean them up, so I would. However, if he was around when they needed to be cleaned up, he would cry in frustration. I didn't understand his unusual behavior or where it came from.

I had dealt with the terrible twos with other children. Robert was much older and the tantrums were much worse. The tantrums never went away and continued to increase in frequency as he aged. I quickly learned to pick my battles, as it was one of the only ways to manage the behavior and cope with my frustration. Many people didn't understand these tantrums are truly part of PWS and not simply bad behavior and so I was often criticized for spoiling him.

Our family ate healthy food. Dinner was eaten as a family, at home, and we didn't eat much fast-food. I spent a lot of time cooking food that was healthy and delicious, trying to manage portion control and calories for Robert. He continued to gain weight so easily. This focus on his caloric intake would create unhealthy behaviors in me, Carey and Cara, as well as our extended family when we got together. When we had snacks and treats, we would hide from Robert in order to conceal the extra treats so he wouldn't fixate on them and want some. Robert was also only allowed one serving of dinner. The rest of us would conceal second helpings while cleaning up; eating over the sink or with our backs to him while he was occupied with something else.

I cook professionally and can make just about anything. I love feeding people the dishes I make. It makes me feel good to see them enjoy my cooking. Sometimes you hear chefs and other professional bakers and cooks say they never cook at home. It's the same as any profession I suppose, you do it all day at work and the last thing you want to do is more of the same work at home. I never felt that way. Perhaps it was because I had my own catering company and worked out of my own kitchen so my "work cooking" was done in the same location as "home cooking'. Either way, cooking has always been a joy and I loved cooking for my family. I still do. How ironic my son, who loved everything I made, could eat so little of it, and I had to so closely manage what he ate. Every night after dinner, Robert would say "really good dinner Mom." It would bring a smile to my face and make me feel a little less guilty about sneaking food when he wasn't looking. Plus, what mother doesn't love hearing compliments from their child?

Outside of laughing with my friends, I got away from life's stresses by riding horses. A high school friend, Sunny, part of the gang, had horses we rode together. Riding kept me in the moment. It was the only exercise where I wasn't preoccupied with what I would cook for lunch or dinner or what would need to take care of next for Robert. It still is the perfect mini-vacation for me. It helps my mind shed all its worries.

Naturally, with my love of horses and the time I spent riding, it didn't take long before I heard of a horse therapy program called We Can Ride for people with physical problems. I know how much riding horses builds my leg strength and core muscles, so it made total sense this could be a great program to strengthen Robert's lower body. It was expensive. Fortunately, Dakota County, where we lived, had a new assistance program that would cover the cost if Robert qualified. The county would give you $1,500 every six months to use for anything you needed. I filled out the paperwork, sent it off, and prayed he qualified for the aid.

Robert was approved. This gave us the funding, and officially registered him as disabled with the state, which would be important moving forward for other programs. We Can Ride was based at The Boys Home School in Minnetonka. The horses were used to both teach delinquent teens responsibility, and as a physical therapy tool for people with special needs.

All the classes we attended were for children. Each child had two side walkers; one to keep them secure, and the other to lead the horse. For those who haven't been around horses and are not familiar with the term, a side walker is just like it sounds, someone who walks alongside the horse next to the rider to aid them should they start to slip or lean away from the horse. Depending upon the child and their physical needs, the horses wear different types of saddles and reins. Some have saddle blankets with handles to hang onto, some have traditional saddles, and others have reins attached to halters. This allows the rider to focus on the muscle group or motor skill they need to strengthen. The horses then walk or trot around an indoor arena, while games are played to encourage riders to stretch and work their muscles while keeping things interesting.

During his second lesson, Robert was encouraged to stand in his stirrups and grab on to the horse's mane. For non-riders, this is the position more advanced riders use while jumping over objects, and certainly works your upper leg and core muscles. Robert was only able to stand up for a second or two before he had to sit back down. It was brief and amazing for me to see. H by the end of the nine-week session Robert was able to go around the whole arena in his jumping position. I couldn't believe it! Watching his progress, my eyes filled with joyful tears, it truly was miraculous.

I saw many more miracles over the years while Robert rode. The leg muscles of children with Cerebral Palsy constrict and need to be stretched. Riding relaxes the muscles without pain. I would stand watching with the other parents behind the gate that separated us. Children's walkers were left behind, as children mounted "their horse." A look of utter joy and freedom shone on their faces and never ceased to amaze and delight me. Even though multiple horseflies would buzz around my head, the smiles, laughter, shrieks of joy and hand clapping, made it all worth it and will stay with me forever.

Robert and I bonded with many of the volunteers. Robert was always chatting with his side walkers, becoming more verbal and engaging. We saw several of the same volunteers' session after session, year after year. They were committed to the program, and all the children it helped. Several riders stayed with the programs as we did and competed in Special Olympic horse shows in later years.

The rest of the family never shared the same love of horses Robert and I had. Carey complained about all the horseflies at the lessons. Initially Cara was also taken with riding lessons. She looked so adorable dressed in paddock boots, breeches, and helmet, with her long blond braid as the perfect accessary. However, her pony bucked during her first show and she was never interested in riding again.

As we looked for more horse riding resources for Robert, an acquaintance of mine allowed us to use her pony. Cara led the pony and I walked alongside. One day she looked at me during Robert's ride and said, "Maybe I'll ride when the pony grows up." Surprised by her statement I replied, "But it's a pony!" Not understanding me, she said, "Yeah I know, when he gets bigger." I couldn't believe she didn't know the difference and replied a bit more forcefully than I intended, "He won't get bigger, he's a pony!" I couldn't understand because I had read everything about horses I could get my hands on when I was her age. I had always been in love with horses and from a young age used to ask my dad to buy me one. This was just another reflection of how different we were in many ways. And another example of my mouth running away from me, inadvertently offending Cara, pushing a wedge between us that would remain throughout her teen years.

Horse therapy was our first foray into therapies outside of traditional physical therapy, and it worked so well I was motivated to try other programs. Courage Center Minnesota offered modified sports programs to people with disabilities. I was eager to try them, much like any parent when their child starts getting involved in sports and other extracurricular activities. The first program we tried was downhill skiing. Carey, Cara and I all loved downhill skiing, and I was thrilled Robert could experience the rush of flying down a snow-clad hill.

We rented equipment for the first lesson. What a struggle it was to get Robert into his boots for the first time. By the time the boots were on I was covered in sweat. Robert was hardly able to take a step in them, "This will never work," I thought. Once again the volunteers proved amazing. They got him out on the hill, into his skis, and up the hill.

The program assisted people who had mental and physical impairments, blind skiers and amputees. I was amazed by the different technology they used to enable the skiers: sleds, chairs, ski bras, etc. The skis Robert used were traditional skis with a ski bra; a metal bar attached to the front keeps the skis parallel or wedge shaped, depending upon what the instructor wants. Then tethers (like reins) were attached to the skis, keeping the instructor always attached to Robert. Of course, it took a village of people to help him. It was also really satisfying to know he was experiencing the same things as a normal child. Cath, my sister, said "Robert skis and rides horses, I don't have a disability but I can't do any of those things!"

We also enrolled Robert in Courage Camp. His first experience was a week-long day camp. I would drop Robert off at eight in the morning and pick him up at three in the afternoon. He loved it and it gave me five hours of freedom on four consecutive days. It also helped get me used to trusting others to take care of Robert. Eventually he stayed at Courage Overnight Camp in Maple Lake, Minnesota for five days.

The Camp had many activities including celebrity visits. One year, Smoky the Bear posed for pictures with the children. Robert was angry another boy was in his picture with Smoky. "Robert," I said, "that little boy didn't have any hands, didn't you feel sad for him?" "I just wanted the picture of me and Smoky, not him," Robert said. Moments like this were hard for me. I couldn't blame Robert for his response, he was simply responding like any young child would when another child did something they didn't like. Sometimes even parents of special needs children forget the difference between their child's emotional age and actual age.

I hoped Robert would make friends at camp because he really didn't have friends at home. Sure he knew kids at his school, and we lived in a kind community where the kids were nice to him in so many ways. He was often unable to participate in the games higher functioning children played. Luckily, Robert wasn't really interested in friendships, which slightly lessened my heartbreak. "Did you make any friends at camp?" I would ask every time he came home. "Oh yes," Robert answered. The friends would always be the camp staff.

Constance's Story

Constance McLeod is a clinical psychologist who worked with special needs children and burn victims at

Gillette hospital for twenty years. I spoke with her about the lack of friends for special needs children. She explained children with special needs spend much more time with adults. They have occupational, physical, and speech therapists, along with personal care attendants or aids (PCA), and, of course, doctors. These are predictable people; other children are not. Children, in general, are happy to see you one moment and punch or pinch you the next. Special needs children are not interested in spending time with unpredictable people. Special needs children also remain egocentric longer than other children, because they are usually the center of attention for the entire household. Many are anxious in social situations, unable to express this feeling. All these things combine to make friendship building with peers a rather daunting task and why it doesn't happen often.

Constance also states many of the problems we face with our children are part of an ongoing power struggle. She encourages parents to use strategies to make the child more responsible and the parents less authoritarian. One example she suggested was making a tape with the child's voice prompting himself to get in the shower. A song can be played for the length of time it takes to shower. The child's own voice then says "Okay, time to get out and dry off." Rewards can be given for sticking to the schedule.

Caring for a special needs child can be exhausting work, both mentally and physically. Courage Center gave our family some of the respite time we needed. Through the years I have listened to parents express frustration and exhaustion. Trusting others to care for your special needs child is vital. They are afraid their child could be abused, or they are afraid to lose control, believing they are the only ones who truly know what their child needs. While I agree as a parent, we know best, it doesn't mean others don't care or understand. I don't advise giving your child to just anyone, if it is a reliable person, say yes. Everyone needs a break, even if it's only for an hour. The time away helps you recharge your batteries and come back a happier, better parent.

OUR FAMILY

CHAPTER EIGHT

EVERYONE NEEDS SOMEONE TO LEAN ON

I've found asking for help is never easy, it makes you vulnerable. Most of us think we should keep our struggles hidden. Never show weakness. Isn't that the American way? When you have a special child your struggles are out there for the world to see. Maybe people can't identify exactly what is going on with your child, still the differences are apparent. We were lucky to have family support. My sisters and brother all lived near me and although she spent several retirement years in sunny California, my Mom moved back shortly after Robert was born to help us. Mom would come over at a moment's notice to baby sit, do the laundry and dishes; helping me cope with the day-to-day needs of the house. She was a gift. My sister Cath (and her husband Dave) and brother Tom, also helped with respite care. They would have one or two of the children over for a weekend stay. Friday became the weekly sleepover night at Auntie and Uncle Dave's house. A shower and nail care was part of the routine. It was no simple feat as Robert hated having his nails clipped. Auntie and Uncle Dave found a way to get it done with success. Dave would always make Robert laugh at the dinner table. Robert slept in Kelly's trundle bed. Kelly read Harry Potter books aloud each time he visited.

These nights were a precious gift for our marriage. We would use the time to go out for dinner and a ballroom dance lesson. After Robert's birth, Carey came home one day with a gift certificate for lessons. Neither of us knew a thing about dancing as a couple. We grew up only dancing to rock and roll. It was something we could learn together, laughing at our mistakes. I think dancing helped us stay married. It also gave me insight into motor memory. Our instructor would teach us a new pattern at each lesson, and we would struggle though the steps. Two weeks later we would breeze though the same steps that had given us such trouble. Without intending it, our dance lessons helped me better understand what the physical therapists always said about Robert. His motor memory was not processing information the same way ours did. His brain did not remember how he had done something the last time. This was exhausting for him, as well as for us. He needed constant cues to navigate the world.

Our family belonged to a big Presbyterian church in St. Paul. Carey's parents had been active members there for many years and had many friends there. Carey and I became active members and both Cara and Robert were baptized in the church and attended the children's programs.

The children's programs were outstanding. Cara and Kelly rehearsed every Wednesday with the children's choir. While the children learned music, mothers gathered at Cafe Latte` on Grand Ave for coffee. This powerful, dynamic, and sympathetic group of women encouraged and supported each other. We laughed at the anecdotes each of us told. We all had so much to say and laugh about we would joke about only being able to speak when the saltshaker was passed. Our spouses had a hard time understanding the group dynamics, "How do you get a word in, or understand each other, when you're all talking over each other?" We couldn't really explain it, instead their confusion just made us laugh even more.

Darlene's Story

One of the great things about belonging to a larger church is there were several ministers who each had specific focus areas of ministry. My church had someone focused on men's ministry and another on women's ministry. Darlene Stensby was the minister focused on women, and she had shepherded several women's programs throughout the years she was caring for the congregation. One such program was called "Women Tell Your Stories," where in a morning meeting, women from the congregation would share stories about their lives. Darlene had an aura of light around her. Her compassion and acceptance of life's joys and hardships made her a powerful role model. She knew how a child's pain could impact a parent, and vice versa. Her family had lost a daughter due to the complications of an eating disorder, so she knew this pain first-hand. I was drawn to Darlene and her women's ministry programs, which were a wonderful resource to help me connect with God and the support system within my congregation. I also began a friendship with Darlene. Our connection continued long after she retired from active ministry.

I also began casually arranged spiritual counseling sessions privately with Darlene. I would go and see her when the pain became too much to bear. During our times together, I would climb the stairs to her beautifully decorated office with a heavy heart. I would sit across from Darlene on the couch in her office on the second floor of the church and pour out my story. My eyes would fill with tears and my nose would run. All of the grief I felt for my imperfect child would pour out. Darlene never had answers and she didn't try to solve my problems. Instead, she would reassure me "God's love is for all of us, imperfect as we all are." She would hold my hands in prayer, and I would be caught up in her beautiful words. During those meetings she prayed specifically for me and my situation. I know many other people in our church were also comforted by her words. It was her calling, and she was truly gifted in this area. Her direct line to God, as I liked to think of it, assured me I was not alone. Since we met only occasionally, I didn't have a standing meeting. And although I sometimes realized I was in need of talking with her, often it was my mom who would encourage me to call and set up a time. "I think it's time you see Darlene again," she would softly encourage.

Reading has always been an important part of my life. It is another way I get away. And I've always loved to read all types of genres, each one fulfilling a need. I love being a part of someone else's life in a novel or thriller, while spiritual books have often uplifted me and encouraged my faith. One book in particular which impacted my life, is called A Course in Miracles by Marianne Williamson. Williamson wrote about how fear steals our lives. How we often talk of being uncomfortable, or unsure of ourselves. Williamson stated, we are just glossing over fear. Fear is our biggest emotion. It colors everything. It steals our energy and changes the way we view the world. Her words certainly hit home for me!

Fear affected my life in a big way. I was afraid for Robert. I was afraid he would not have any friends and would not do well in school. I was constantly preoccupied with fear in the form of questions. Would Robert start gaining weight faster as he got older? Would we have to lock our refrigerator and cupboards? What would his behavior be tomorrow, one year from now, five years from now? Would I ever have to watch my child so frenzied with the need for food that he was digging through the garbage like I'd read about PWS victims? None of these questions ever got answered, they just took me away from being present in the moment and continued to churn and increase the size of the knot permanently residing in my stomach.

Although most of the time I was a stay-at-home mom and Carey was the breadwinner, I did open and run my own small catering company, thanks to a dear friend's mother, who basically started having me work for her and her friends. This allowed my income to cover the many additional needs of our household. When Robert was young, I already had several years under my belt and was used to catering parties. Soon, the anxiety and fear I had for Robert began spilling into my work life as well. I felt preoccupied and sick with worry before events even started. The parties I'd catered in the past got rave reviews, during this time period, before every party, I was sure something would go wrong. I learned first-hand fear makes a challenging job much harder.

After reading Marianne Williamson's book, I vowed to change. I told myself I would give Robert the best possible life I could, and I would let the rest go. I also told myself parties were not life and death events. If I failed to make the perfect dessert or entre', the world would not end. In fact, life would go on, and most of the partygoers wouldn't even notice. Identifying fear and knowing its effects, made it less powerful. I vowed to always remember that, and to take deep breaths to calm myself. I also continued my practice of taking a rest in the middle of the day when Robert was napping, or the kids were in school. So many cultures implement this practice, even within the working world, and their work-life-spiritual balance is better than ours. I also focused on being grateful and happy with what I had. These are all things we have heard, to practice them, takes real determination.

Marianne Williamson also stated in her book, "abundance is available to everyone." There is enough love to go around. I thought this was such an important and crucial idea, and I still do. I've also found sometimes I'm too eager to share these ideas and "fix" a problem. Shortly after I read her book and started making changes in my behavior, I said to Cara, "just because I love Kelly doesn't mean there is less love for you." I thought by sharing this idea with Cara I could make her young mind (she was only ten or so at the time) understand this important concept, which I thought would be so helpful. I thought what a huge benefit it would have been if I'd known as a teenager. Then again, it's easy to say I would have seen it that way then, as I'm thinking through my adult lens now. Because instead of spurring a conversation with Cara, she responded rather indignantly, "Does that mean you love her more than me?!" Why did I always think I needed to share these ideas, particularly with my young daughter? She wasn't ready to handle these concepts; it needed to be enough they helped me.

ROBERT WITH GRANDMA

CHAPTER NINE

FINALLY GETTING AN ANSWER

The clinic visits we had started at Gillette continued on an on-going basis for Robert at three-month intervals. At age seven we had a monumental appointment. A new test for the detection of PWS had been developed in Rochester. Dr. Ainslie informed us about the test, and said the lab would take blood for the testing procedure. We had operated for several years with a diagnosis of PWS-like, it hadn't been truly official. Not having a definitive answer to what Robert was dealing with would not change his care, or who he was, and it felt like this was our chance to finally have a real answer to the questions Carey and I had carried since Robert's tumultuous birth.

Robert hated any kind of needles. It was a phobia he developed early on from so many clinic visits. Of course this made getting any laboratory procedures done, or administering a shot an ordeal. Part of me wishes Dr. Ainslie hadn't mentioned we needed to take blood for the test, it was a perfectly normal thing to say when describing this new test. However, for Robert, having that inform-ation during the doctor visit only heightened his anxiety. When we took an elevator down to the lab floor Robert stated, "I think we should reschedule." Starting in a somewhat calm and normal tone he continued to say "I think we should reschedule," in a louder voice each time he said it. By the time we reached the lab and checked in, he was screaming "I think we should reschedule!" at the top of his voice. Two lab techs hustled him back into the lab immediately. They had to hold him down while he continued to scream throughout the entire process. I suppose, over the years, I've turned this into a comical story I share with friends. Truthfully, it's heartbreaking to see your child in situations where you feel absolutely helpless to comfort them or make them understand why something needs to happen.

Once our traumatic lab experience was over, we went home and didn't find out the results for another three months. "The test came back positive," Dr. Ainslie informed us, "Robert does have Prader-Willi." My stomach had been churning all morning before the appointment. Now I felt sick at heart and overwhelmed with grief. Denial is a great comfort in so many ways. Before we had a confirmed diagnosis of PWS it was easy to rationalize Robert's behavior, not really thinking about what the future had in store. Now we knew it was PWS, all I could think about was the fact my child would die at a young age from complications of obesity. It seemed unbearable. "You'll get through this," my mom reassured me as we left the hospital that day. I wasn't sure how. What I soon realized was while the diagnoses impacted the entire family in many ways, it didn't really change our day-to-day life.

Daniel's Story

Daniel's PWS was diagnosed at age four by a syndromologist (physician concerned with the taxonomy, etiology, and patterns of congenital malformations). Daniel is five years older than Robert and was diagnosed in 1988, eight years before we received Robert's PWS confirmation. Neil, Daniel's father, a very analytical person, said "he was happy to know what it was from an early age." His reaction was the exact opposite of mine. Where I wanted to deny the doctors prognosis, and honestly did, for the first seven years of Robert's life, Neil welcomed knowing what Daniel was dealing with.

Daniel is the baby of the family. He has a good relationship with his older brother. Neil and his wife were lucky to have had few problems between them as the boys grew up. Daniel is especially close to his mom and when he was young he used to say "I'm never leaving home," because he couldn't think of a time he'd want to live without her nearby.

Perhaps it was due to having such an early diagnosis and Neil being so analytical they were able to prepare so well for the traits of the syndrome. Or perhaps Daniel is just one of those PWS kids who's had fewer complications with his traits. His father reiterated the Mayo Clinic diagnosis confirmation helped them focus on Daniel's needs. Straight away Neil and his wife created a structured environment for Daniel where they kept food locked up. They believe the controlled setting decreased his anxiety and helped him get along well with friends and do well in school. Daniel's family have been active participants of PWSA MN. Neil served as board president for several years.

CHAPTER TEN

SHOWING MORE TRAITS OF THE SYNDROME

Shortly after the confirmed PWS diagnosis, Robert developed more traits of the syndrome. His temper tantrums increased as well as obsessive compulsive behaviors. It was hard to admit I was wrong about his diagnosis all along. I realize now the benefit of knowing is priceless; you can't fight something you don't know. Prader-Willi is a complicated syndrome. The people affected have a drive for food that is never satisfied. Their mind is always focused on food. I had dealt with my share of body-image related eating issues (as so many females do) and I still struggle with them. Having Robert so focused on food, I decided to try to manage food by focusing on portion control. Counting calories just seemed too hard. Today there are so many amazing apps, and the calories are even listed at restaurants. When Robert first started showing signs of needing stricter food management, the technology wasn't available. I didn't want my life to become solely focused on calorie intake either, so by keeping his portions controlled, never using food as a reward, and sparingly giving Robert treats, I tried my best to manage his weight.

Often I had to say "not today buddy," when he'd want something more, it seemed so much better than saying "you know you can't have that." The promise of tomorrow seemed to satisfy him a lot of the time. We also never had to lock food away. Robert knew the cupboards and refrigerator were not to be opened and he never did. This was a blessing, particularly in light of having my home-based catering company. I realize Robert is more unique in this respect, many PWS kids would not have been able to obey these rules. I do have to stress this strategy worked well in Robert's younger years, likely wouldn't be consistently successful now he is an adult.

We continued to walk and do other forms of exercise to try to make sure Robert was getting as much movement in as possible. Robert was a slow walker though. His short legs never responded to my prompts of "can you go a little faster?" I've told friends I would be a millionaire today if they gave out nickels for repeating this phrase. Patience was never my strong suit, I often thought God was teaching me a lesson on these walks, as there never was a way to hurry Robert along.

During our walks I would find myself several paces in front of Robert. Turning around, I would repeat "can you go a little faster?" Robert's gait would increase for a few steps and then he'd return to his slow stroll. I was forced to learn patience, literally one step at a time. Life's lessons are presented over and over until we get it, often taught through things we don't think of as important, or even necessary.

The neighborhood school Cara and Robert attended, Mendota Elementary, was outstanding. Robert was mainstreamed and had a para-professional working with him in class for the majority of the day. He was only pulled out of class for speech and physical therapy.

Robert knew the names of all the teachers and office workers. His memory for names is really extraordinary. He would ride a trike around the hall during physical therapy for exercise, and as he passed each person would greet them by name and ask "How are you today?"

We often missed school for appointments at Gillette. Growth hormones were just starting to be used to treat stature and growth issues for children with PWS. Dr. Ainslie, was one of the first doctors to recommend it. He even spoke of it and encouraged growth hormone use at a PWS conference. Dr. Willi, a discoverer of the syndrome, was also in attendance at the conference, he did not share Dr. Ainslie's enthusiasm for the drug. It was not readily available at the time and it didn't help every patient. He felt these were significant barriers to being a valuable treatment option.

In general, growth hormones help a PWS child grow taller and promote lean body mass. (Butler p.206-207) They are shown to help some patients with certain behaviors and cognitive skills. Dr. Ainslie recommended Robert try them. A one-month supply cost $3,000.00, out-of-pocket. Our insurance covered the cost only after we paid our $1,500.00 deductible each year. We decided the possible benefits were worth the price, and certainly realized the huge advantage we had in only having to pay four percent of the out-of-pocket costs for a one-year supply.

Serena's Story

Serena who is now 29 was also offered Growth Hormones. At the time she was also taking insulin for diabetes. Her parents felt the extra Growth Hormone injection was more than their daughter could handle. Serena was getting about four injections a day. The science that recommends GH today was not available then. Newly diagnosed babies with PWS are often given GH at a very young age. Serena, now lives in a group home that restricts calories and exercises regularly is now totally off insulin. She gets a small dose of GH six days a week. Serena loves to do artwork and makes her housemates beautiful cards for their birthdays.

Growth hormones helped improve Roberts strength muscle mass and height. He continued to gain too much weight. Scoliosis can also be a potential problem for people with PWS and growth hormones can exacerbate Scoliosis, because the child's bones and muscle mass grow more rapidly than normal. To help manage this risk, another doctor was added to the list of people we saw at Gillette. Originally from South Africa, with a charming accent, Dr. L., is an orthopedic surgeon specializing in the spine. He diagnosed a curve in Robert's spine and suggested we start bracing his back to try slowing the progression of the scoliosis.

Gillette's Assisted Technology department began the process of creating his brace by making a plaster model of Robert's body. From the plaster model they created a plastic vest with Velcro straps which kept the brace in place. I recall laughing when one of the technologists said "there's a lot of tissue to deal with here," as he began the process of creating the plaster model. I know he wasn't trying to make a mean comment about Robert, as a PWS mom you're already so worried about their size, when someone brings it up, it's easy to take offense.

Once Robert started wearing the vest, we were back to Gillette for adjustments constantly. Robert wore wear the vest day and night, 24 hours a day, or until it started to hurt and he requested a break. A lack of sensitivity to pain is another facet of PWS, so complaints about the vest didn't always come forward as quickly as they would from a normal child wearing a similar brace. Robert's sensitivity was so low; he was never able to feel if his shoes were too tight.

Our appointments for adjustments were generally in the morning. Then I would let him have a small lunch at Burger King before going back to school. It became one more routine we couldn't deviate from. When Cara and Kelly were little, any doctor or dentist visit always ended in a treat if they were good. For them, seeing the doctor was a fairly rare occurrence. And like so many other parents do, as they reached school age, the treat often turned into lunch before bringing them back to school, because they'd miss lunch otherwise. I remember initially doing this with

Robert too, how could I not do the same for each of my children. Burger King was not a good choice for someone with the syndrome I realized too late. Robert was entrenched in his routine and we could never leave the doctor's office without stopping for lunch without a huge meltdown.

ROBERT WITH UNCLE TOM, KELLY, AND CARA

CHAPTER ELEVEN

ELEMENTARY SCHOOL FRIENDSHIPS AND TRANSITIONING TO MIDDLE SCHOOL

Like so many communities based on school districts, many of the children Robert went to school with in kindergarten were part of his life through senior year. We had so many good experiences—families were kind; some even began inviting Robert to birthday parties.

One party in elementary school was held at a roller rink. When I called to decline I told the parents "Robert can't skate." They said, "That's okay, please come anyway, we're bringing games for him to play." Another family we met through school, the Vans, had playdates (AKA babysat for us) and gave Carey and me the gift of time away. The Vans always had vanilla ice cream with chocolate sauce as a treat after dinner, so Robert loved going there.

The hard part for any mother watching her child grow up is worrying if they'll have friends and be liked. We want our children to be happy and content. This is even more difficult when you have a special needs child. Robert had imaginary friends and was a hero in his own mind, in his imaginary world. He never thought of himself as somehow less than anyone else. He chose to be friends with the highest achievers at school; or maybe they chose to be kind and make friends with him. Recalling his day camp experience, he was always friends with the counselors, because they did all the work in the friendship.

As Robert aged, these children had less and less time to spend with him and it became difficult to arrange playdates. Instead of the normal give and take between moms, I would be the person to set everything up. Of course I can't blame these children, they were growing up and interested in age-appropriate games and pastimes, Robert was still very young emotionally. I began to arrange playdates with younger children of family friends who were still interested in Nintendo DS and Pokémon, Robert's favorite companions.

Of course, it was painful to see other boys his age riding bikes together or playing basketball. My childhood had been spent playing outdoors with neighborhood friends as had Cara's, that was never part of Robert's childhood experience. These feelings are part of an ongoing grieving process I've found, at least for me, has become less intense with the passing years, yet never goes away completely.

Grief comes in many forms. I have no patience for articles I read that put too positive a spin on parenting a special needs child. The actor parent of a Down syndrome child stated, "It took six weeks to adjust and then everything was a joy." Another person stated on social media, "Meeting an autistic person will change your life forever." Autistic people are individuals; some are enjoyable others are not.

It is totally ridiculous in my opinion, to simplify such complicated issues. This is not what we signed up for when we became parents. Of course you love your children, you don't foresee taking care of them for the rest of your life. Your child's siblings have to become caretakers some point. These are problems are processed over a lifetime, not six weeks.

Robert never took the short bus, as it is called. He was always picked up and dropped off in front of our house, it was the same bus all the elementary children rode. The drivers encouraged Robert to sit in front, he preferred the back for some reason. The other children in the neighborhood waited impatiently for him to walk down the aisle and then navigate the stairs.

I would tell him every day before he got on the bus, "Your imaginary friends can't go to school with you today." To which he would reply, "I tell them that, Mom, somehow they always get on the bus, they are Power Rangers after all." Imaginary friends became a big part of his life. Robert continued to play with string or his sister's old jump rope. He would sit in a chair dangling the rope in front of him, talking in a soft voice. I was the one who was sad about his lack of real life connections and friendships, I don't think he was.

Mendota Elementary School only went through fourth grade. When Robert graduated, the longtime principal was also leaving, so a program to honor him was planned. Speeches were made, songs were sung, it was all very emotional. At the end of the program a mic was made available to anyone who had something to say. Robert raised his hand and was handed the mic while I held my breath.

Robert began with his history at Mendota, naming his teachers in chronological order, as well as the staff, Robert stated how much he loved the school, the principal, and the students. There wasn't a dry eye in the house. Many parents came up to me afterward and complimented Robert's speech.

The transition to Friendly Hills Middle school was extremely difficult. Routine is so important to many PWS children and Robert was no different. Moving to a new school with a very different layout and daily schedule was a huge disruption in his routine. Robert continued to be mainstreamed at this point and had a para-professional for part of the day. His fifth grade teacher was a wonderful person, new to teaching. It was clear having Robert in the class was a big stress for the teacher. I received many phone calls regarding Robert's behavior at the beginning of the school year.

I began to see Robert was becoming a master manipulator. I warned teachers, staff, family friends, anyone who spent consistent time with him saying, "He will manipulate you so well you will feel good about it." It's hard to say things like this about your child, I recognized what was happening and wanted to prevent issues before they surfaced.

One such example centered around homework. Being mainstreamed meant Robert had to keep up with the work his classmates were doing. Homework, and sometimes additional homework, was necessary if he couldn't finish his in-class work during the day. Instead of having a conversation between myself and the teacher to discuss this (again, the teacher was new to teaching) he took Robert at his word when Robert stated I liked helping him with homework.

In reality, we would spend two hours or more a night trying to get homework done between tears and outbursts. When I realized the volume of homework was not easing up, I contacted the social worker at school because of Robert's independent education plan. I left an angry voicemail stating my unhappiness about the excessive amount of homework. Instead of calling me back and talking with me and/or the teacher, the social worker played the voicemail for Robert. "See how unhappy you are making your mother," he said. He probably thought he was shaming Robert into behavior change, I don't know for sure. When Robert came home to tell me about the voicemail he told me he was so sad to hear my voicemail. Although I realize I shouldn't have left such an emotionally charged voicemail and should have waited to call until I was calmer, I was dumbfounded and irate to think a professional social worker would do something so unethical. My next call was to the principal of the school.

A meeting was quickly set up with the director of special education. The social worker apologized, the director apologized, and a new strategy and independent education plan was created. The resource room, staffed with a special education teacher and para-professionals, were now going to be a big part of Robert's day. He was no longer was able to keep up in a mainstream setting. It was time to transition to a full-time special needs education approach.

Mrs. Barnes, the special education teacher, was our salvation. She quickly implemented a program that worked well for Robert. School became a place where small successes were achieved though repetition and one-on-one supervision. I was grateful to be over the initial turmoil we experienced at the beginning of the year. Middle School now became a stable place. The resource room would be Robert's home base though Middle School. I was so blown away by what Mrs. Barnes did for Robert, and all the children in her class, I entered her in a Teacher of the Year Award contest. I wrote a letter saying how much Mrs. Barnes had helped our family and she won the contest! She was able to use the prize money toward her master's degree.

CHAPTER TWELVE

SCOLIOSIS THROWS US A CURVE

In middle school, Robert's health became a bigger problem. He had been taking growth hormone injections since the third grade, and had gained considerable height, causing the curve in his spine to become more pronounced. We knew the risk when it was first suggested as a treatment, and we knew Robert had some spinal curve since Dr. L. had required Robert wear a brace continuously since he started the injections. We weren't shocked to find it was necessary to do something more than continue with the brace.

Robert's curve was 97 degrees at the top of the spine and 95 degrees at the bottom, almost a perfect S. Dr. L. felt it was time for a full spinal fusion. The surgery involved placing a titanium rod though Robert's spine. It would be anchored with screws and bone taken from Robert's hip. The bone from the hip would be ground to form a paste. "Without it", Dr. L. said, "the spine will bend the titanium rod." How amazing our bones are stronger than titanium.

Scoliosis is quite common for people with PWS and can be either mild or severe. Screening should be an essential part of their health care, surgery can be problematic because of the threat of respiratory compromise and infection. Robert's case was so severe we had to trust Dr. L. advice and proceed with surgery.

After surgery Robert would no longer need the vest he had worn day and night for almost three years. We would no longer have to visit the Assisted Technology department for continual adjustments. These were positive things in my mind, yet I worried, wondering if he would fully recover and be able to walk again.

The surgery began early in the morning and lasted for seven hours. Our family and friends visited with us during the day. Dr. L. came to tell us the good news. "The surgery went well," he said. "The curve in the spine is much improved, 47 degrees on top and 43 degrees on the bottom." This was significant. Scoliosis patients can typically never return to zero degrees of curvature, so to have the surgery reduce the curve in Robert by more than half was incredibly successful.

We were overwhelmed with gratitude. We waited another two hours while they sutured the incision, and another hour with Robert in post-op before we were able to see our boy. The emotional roller coaster we had been on all day exhausted us all. After a short visit with Robert, we went home to sleep for a few hours. While we were at home, my mom and Cath stayed at the hospital so Robert would have family there if something came up. When we came back to the hospital later in the evening, they greeted us in the hallway, Mom told us, and "He is fine and resting comfortably." We said our goodbyes as they went home for the night and we went into intensive care.

We made it into Robert's room to find him becoming increasingly agitated. He was trying to remove his oxygen tube, and a sensor was alerting the staff to his shallow breathing. Although Robert's behavior change wasn't totally surprising, it was alarming. At the same moment, a real emergency was happening two doors down when they called a code blue. The staff started moving in and out of the room quickly. The nurses were able to take care of Robert's agitation quickly and he settled back down, we were shaken after witnessing the action down the hall and wondering if the little boy or girl was going to be okay or not. I prayed for that child and their family hoping everything turned out all right.

We spent most of the next week at the hospital while Robert recovered. Cath came by daily and during one visit gave Robert his bed bath. It took her three hours, with Robert offering no help. She never complained, after all, she is always Robert's faithful nurse and auntie.

On day two a nurse came in to get Robert out of bed and moving around a little. I was sitting behind him in a chair, so as he got out of the bed his open gown allowed me to view his entire incision. Seeing the whole length of your child's spine closed only by sutures was difficult for me. I felt light-headed and sick. Meanwhile, the nurse continued to urge Robert to sit up and get out of bed. Normally this would be the time I would step in and assist to get Robert to do what needed to be done. However, at the moment, I was no help. I was still trying to recover from the sight of my baby boy's incision. I kept thinking "if I had an incision that long I wouldn't want to get out of bed either!

It took two hours of urging to get Robert to stand. Again, I have to stress how wonderful it is to have a hospital like Gillette which works with special needs children specifically, and shows endless patience with them. By the end of the week Robert was walking the halls and going up and down stairs. We were able to rent a hospital bed for the lower level of our house, and so after a seven-day stay, he was discharged and we took him home to finish his healing in his own environment.

We were blessed to have had so much support from family and friends. Meals and gifts were dropped off, all of which made my life so much easier. My mom would stay whenever I worked and help me with the house. Just having the laundry and dishes done gave me a few extra moments in my day. This helped reduce some stress, I moved through life in a state of agitation, completely preoccupied with what needed to be done for Robert.

It took many weeks, the incision was healing beautifully and Robert was more and more mobile, and getting back to his regular routine. Things were starting to settle down except for the part of the incision near the base of the spine. It was taking longer to heal than the other areas of his back, and Robert started picking at the scab. Picking can be another aspect of PWS. Although we hadn't seen him do it regularly before, it was very concerning now. We did everything possible to get him to stop the picking, it never seemed to totally stop. I worried constantly about infection and what it would ultimately mean for his recovery. After what felt like forever, the area healed. We all finally let out a big sigh of relief.

ME AND ROBERT

CHAPTER THIRTEEN

TIMES OF TRANSITION

The summer the days just seemed to fly. Robert and I walked every day as Dr. L. recommended. It was always slow going, with me urging Robert to walk at a faster pace. As I've mentioned before, during these walks I often felt like grabbing his arm to make him go faster. Instead, I worked on learning patience, it's still a life lesson I haven't completely mastered.

Cara and Kelly both graduated from high school. Cara had continued to struggle with the drama surrounding Robert throughout high school. There was probably a lot more acting out and rebellion by Cara during that period than there would have been if she hadn't had a special needs brother. As they say, any attention is better than none. Cara didn't do anything drastic, she was really a good kid. It came as no surprise after graduation Cara was ready to be on her own and away from all the family drama. She took a job near the Canadian border at the Gunflint Lodge in Grand Marais for the summer, a six-hour drive from our home. She then came back to town and attended Inver Hills Community College in the fall before transferring to North Dakota State the following year. Kelly spent the summer at home and also spent a week at the Gunflint Lodge with Cara before she went off to the University of Minnesota. Although she was technically only 20 minutes away, she lived on campus and the whole family gave her the space she needed to really have the college experience. Cara and Kelly would always stay close and support each other. We missed having them around, they had done so much for Robert; they'd been his playmates, his protectors and his babysitters. We recognized the days of being able to depend on them to watch Robert were over. It was their time to live independent lives, experience life, and find themselves.

Meanwhile, my mom could no longer afford the townhouse she lived in with a roommate, and she needed to move into assisted living. She fought the idea, eventually she agreed and realized it was the right decision. We were planning on picking out new carpet on the afternoon of Monday, August 13. Robert and I were home doing our morning routine when I received a call from the police around noon asking if Merlyn Maroney was my mother. "Yes she is," I said rather confused. "She died today from a heart attack," the officer replied. I was so shocked. Not my mother! She may have smoked yet she was a vital eighty! I replied, "No. No. We were going to pick out carpet today!" I cried. I'm sure officers deal with a lot of shock and grief, so he ignored my distress and simply stated, "We need you to come down to her townhouse."

Robert and I immediately got in the car and drove the seven-minute route to her house. When we walked in the door, she was lying on the floor with the intubation tube still in her mouth. The paramedics had tried to revive her. I sat on the floor next to her and Robert sat in a chair nearby. My mom was the first dead person I had ever seen outside a funeral home. I sobbed and said, "No! No! No!" over and over again. I had never felt such acute grief. Robert cried along with me, he so loved his grandma.

I had to tell my two sisters, brother, Carey, and Cara the news. It was the saddest day of my life. Mom was my greatest cheerleader and support. I know my other family members felt the same way. A future without Mom seemed impossible. My faith helps me know I will see her again someday; I still miss her every day.

Grief makes you do things you wouldn't ordinarily do. Robert knew Cath's home phone number and often liked to call his auntie. I don't recall telling him to call her, her daughter Kelly told me later on that afternoon she was home with her dad, while Cath was at work. She heard the phone ring and just missed it. Retrieving the voicemail, she was completely shaken hearing Robert say in a calm voice, "Auntie where are you? Grandma is dead. Come here now." Kelly cried out to her dad and repeated the message. Dave quickly called the nursing home where Cath worked and told her to get over to her mom's immediately. Kelly and Dave jumped in the car and headed over too. If I'd been in my right mind I know I wouldn't have asked Robert to make any of those calls, he was much too young. I'm glad he made them, because soon the whole family was together, which was exactly where we needed to be.

My mom had what people call a good death. Mom rarely went to a doctor for herself and because of this had untreated high blood pressure. She died instantly of a massive coronary. She never had to leave her home and depend on others. This was a gift because being a burden was one of her greatest fears. However not being able to say goodbye tore at all our hearts. For the first time in my life I was unable to eat. Food had always been one of my greatest comforts, now it was even hard to swallow. I had a constant lump in my throat.

It was a difficult time of transition with Kelly and Cara growing up and then the world seemed to stop on 9/11, just one month after Mom left us. Cath dealt with her grief by saying, "she was certain Mom was busy helping those suddenly dead people transition to the spirit world."

My mom's death triggered a long-lasting depression. Looking back, I am sure depression has been a part of my life for a long time. I just didn't recognize it. Anti-depressants help, getting the dosage right is hard. Too much and you can't cry. Too little and you're still depressed. Regular exercise has helped me a lot, never completely curing my depression it certainly helped me cope with it. Swimming, horseback riding, walking and biking, all seem more like fun than hard work. Often, I had to force myself to work out, when I did I felt better afterwards.

Robert has a spiritual side to his personality. He was always willing to talk about missing his Grandma. He has a very strong belief system and is sure Grandma is with God. He talked about how she liked to ignore his lower calorie diet. "Grandma always made creamed corn for me," he would say, or, "Grandma would put both butter and mayo on a sandwich."

It took my family time to get my Mom's affairs in order; getting everything settled was hard. She owned a small cabin in addition to her town house. My sister Cath and I decided to keep it. It became a weekend retreat of laughter, boating, swimming, and sharing meals. We've always been happy we kept it. Having time there helped ease the pain of grief for all of us. Cath and I could feel our Mom when we were there and we were comforted by her presence.

Robert was always able to keep busy at his grandma's cabin. It was located on a weedy lake. Robert contributed by pulling weeds and placing them on the dock. He could take as much time as he needed and got paid for the effort. His OCD personality traits made this the perfect job for him.

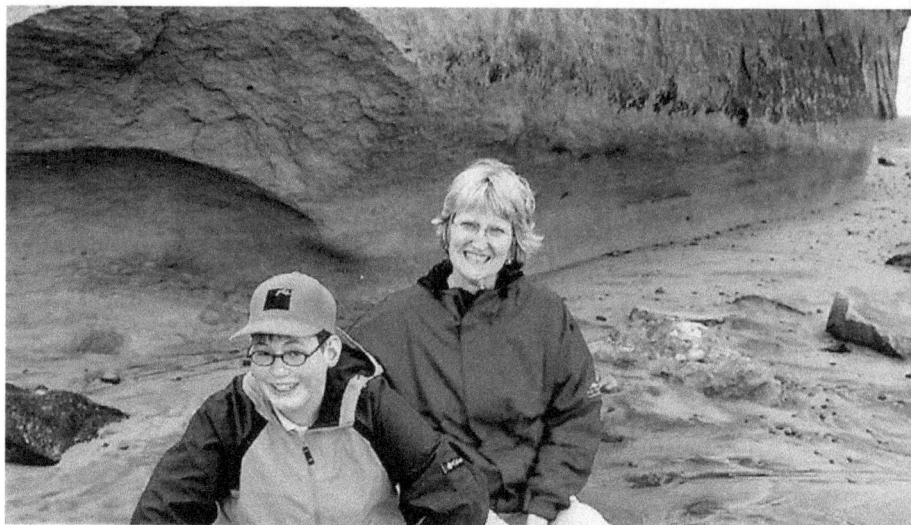

ROBERT WITH AUNTIE CATH

CHAPTER FOURTEEN

MIDDLE SCHOOL TRANSITIONS TO

HIGH SCHOOL

The years in middle school passed quickly. Robert was our only child at this point, now Cara was off at school, along with her cousins. He was actually able to stay alone for up to two hours at a time. Although we didn't do it often, it gave him a sense of independence to be just like everyone else his age. The food-seeking behaviors we had read about hadn't manifested at this point, which made leaving him unsupervised for small periods more possible.

Barbara Whitman who has a Ph.D. in pediatrics wrote the academic article Understanding and Managing the Behavioral Components of Prader-Willi Syndrome. In the article she gives examples of people with PWS ordering 100 pizzas at once or buying $400.00 worth of candy with credit cards. These examples were hard for our family to believe; it did explain how food-driven PWS can make people. We were extremely lucky. We never had to lock up our food the way so many PWS families do. Robert never took any food that wasn't given to him at home. Dr. Ainslie suggested the possibly, with his higher calorie diet, Robert didn't have such a strong food drive. But, if we were to decrease his calories to the recommended 1,400 calories a day, his food drive could increase.

Robert participated in church activities including choir and confirmation. Part of becoming a confirmed church member required Robert to take part in Sunday services on a quarterly basis. At the beginning of the Sunday service, the children would carry a cross or a flag and process into the church with the ministers. The cross was heavy and unwieldy; it would have been easier for Robert to carry a flag. Robert was stubborn and loved his routines. He decided the cross was what he needed to carry, and he would never let anyone else carry it for him. When the procession started, he would slowly walk down the aisle, the cross held high. When he got to the lectern steps a classmate would be there to help him, carry the cross, walk down the aisle, up six stairs, and then stand facing the congregation while the rest of the procession of choir members and readers passed by. Robert had a hard time going up and down the steps alone, so carrying the cross while going up the steps was almost impossible. Every quarterly Sunday during high school I held my breath as he processed into church. It always worked out fine and the other children were always kind and helpful. Church members and friends would often come up to me after the service and tell me how he touched their hearts with his determination.

Robert also had chores he was responsible for, like clearing his dinner plate and picking up toys. Dog walking was also one of Robert's chores. We had a small King

Charles Spaniel named Charley who had no problem with slow strolls around the neighborhood. Charley had a special connection with Robert. During outbursts and tantrums, Charley would jump into Robert's lap and lick his tears away. This never stopped the tantrum, although it seemed to shorten the duration. It would force Robert to hold Charley close. Charley never stopped trying to comfort his friend. During their daily walks, Robert and Charley would stop and visit with neighbors along the way. The stories Robert came back with astonished me. Neighbors would tell him all about their lives, including stories about the family dog or complicated adoptions. Robert was always a good listener. And everyone enjoys being around a good listener.

Robert had strong routines and fixations. We ate meals at regular times and had fruit and vegetables for snacks. Robert ate the same breakfast every day, if he became too fixated on an idea, he was sent to his room. Fixations can often involve transitions from one place to another, even something as simple as a haircut. Robert hated haircuts, especially ones involving a clipper. Sometimes I would bribe him by offering to buy him a coffee if he complied. This is not ideal for PWS. Robert would cry all the way to the salon, and then he would scream and cry himself to sleep. If getting him a coffee could prevent this once in a while, I could rationalize the bribe.

I am sure people who have no experience with PWS think, what a mean mom. What's important to understand is a person with PWS will not change their mind, no matter how many logical arguments you present. Think of trying to tell a two-year-old why they can't have candy at the store. It never works. They are too young to understand, and they are only focused on what they want. This is the mindset of a PWS person because they don't typically mature much past this stage. So it's as if they are always emotionally toddlers, even though they are physically the size of adults.

In her article about PWS, Whitman wrote of the anxiety people with PWS have about food. They think about ways to get more food all the time. I wasn't aware of this aspect of PWS until years later. Although Robert was experiencing anxiety and it can cause many of the behaviors associated with PWS I had never heard of the anxiety piece, and because Robert didn't have the food seeking behaviors, it never occurred to me any of his behaviors were associated with food anxiety

Robert's fascination with food was very much like an eating disorder, and his preoccupation with food did not differ from my own. I thought about food all the time. I was either planning meals for clients or meals for the family. Often addicts refocus their addictive personalities on another substance. As a person living in recovery finding balance with substances is hard. You eliminate one addiction then find another to take its place. Ice cream and chocolate comforted me. The cravings I had for drugs and alcohol diminished, I still thought about ice cream every day.

An example of Robert's oppositional behavior occurred one Sunday evening when we drove to Courage Center for a swim class. Foolishly, I had told Robert 7th Heaven, one of his favorite TV shows, would be over when we got back home. "I wanted to watch my show," he said. "You can't watch it tonight. Next Sunday I'll record it, okay?" I responded. He just kept repeating the same phrase, "I wanted to watch my show," as we got ready for class. I thought he would forget about it once he was in the pool because he loved to swim. No way. As I took my seat in the lobby, he began screaming "I don't want to swim, I want to watch my show!" I went back and told his swim instructors, "Don't engage him, maybe he will let it go." He couldn't move past it and we eventually ended the lesson early and left. Although I'd seen other children have plenty of meltdowns at Courage Center, I was glad there were no other students in the class that night. Of course, he still did not get to watch his show, but, unlike other children who might learn from their tantrums and punishments, Robert never changed his behavior and continued to have tantrums in the future.

I don't want it to sound like Robert was always throwing tantrums, he could also be funny and a true delight to be around. When we decided to participate in a Special Olympic horse show, there were several classes for both English and Western styles. One class had only one competitor--Robert. When he was awarded the gold medal he remarked "I had an injury last year and couldn't compete. This year I decided to go for the gold!" I laughed and asked, "What injury? He replied, "Oh you know, I had a twisted ankle last summer."

Julie, part of our Mendota Elementary group of friends, has four children. Her boys often came over and played video games with Robert. She enjoys recounting an incident which happened at the movie theater while we were together. During an outing to the movies, I had allowed Robert to get Skittles for a treat, but, when he tried to open the Skittles candy the bag suddenly broke apart and scattered all over the floor. He was furious and shrieked, "I am going to sue the maker of Skittles for making the bag so hard to open!" I was already laughing when the candy spilled, and Julie joined me after hearing Robert threaten a lawsuit. Once we pulled ourselves together, I picked up the bag, there was enough candy left in the bag to placate Robert. He was never allowed to have a whole bag, so this eliminated the argument we would have had if he hadn't spilled some.

As it became time to transition to high school, routines needed to be changed again, which was always a struggle. And the high school was a much larger world for Robert to navigate. His high school, Henry Sibley, had a department to teach life skills. Much like middle school, Robert spent the majority of his day in the resource room. Robert and the other special needs students would spend much of their day there. They would not be in class as often with the other students. Carey and I worried about bullying in a larger student setting. It never happened. Maybe we were just lucky to have Robert grow up in a great community. Many of the kids had known him from preschool and were used to him. Or maybe the school just had an exceptionally fine group of professionals who seemed to be caring and understanding of special needs kids. Or, maybe it was simply the egocentric aspect of PWS protecting him, keeping him from being aware of bullying. For Robert, his world continued to focus around his Nintendo DS, Power Rangers and his imaginary super hero friends. Whatever the reason, Robert was happy and I was too.

High school started at seven am, much earlier than middle school, which was yet another change in Robert's routine. In order to get him off to school on time, I had to get Robert up at five am. His compulsive behaviors had continued to increase over the years. Morning showers now took 30 minutes, even with my continued prompts to "Get out of the shower now!" TV was never allowed in the morning, as breakfast was usually an hour long affair. The last 30 minutes we'd rush through teeth brushing, trying to get him in the car and dropped off at school on time. I drove Robert to school; he was never ready in time for the bus.

All the way through high school, we continued with Special Olympics and We Can Ride. Robert rode horseback in the fall, swam and played poly hockey during the winter months. Poly hockey is played indoors on a gym floor, using a modified hockey stick, and the players were special needs kids. Poly Hockey games consisted of the ball being hit toward one of the goals, while the majority of players were looking the opposite way. Much like any game toddlers first play (soccer, baseball, basketball) it's more like herding cats than anything else. It made me laugh to watch Robert and his friends play, I was usually the only one. "Why doesn't anyone else think this is funny?!" I'd think. I suppose political correctness can keep us from enjoying life. It wasn't that I was laughing at the players, not in the least. They were all so joyful to be out there and I took joy in watching the antics ensue. If you can't find joy in things, what's the point? Perhaps, because I've lived through cancer, my mother's death, and other heartbreak and devastation, I've learned life is to be enjoyed. And the best medicine is laughing through the pain.

Patty's Story

My friend Jenny from Mendota Elementary introduced me to Patty. Patty had a daughter, Holly, who was five years younger than Robert and also had special needs. Although she didn't have PWS, some of her behaviors mimicked Robert's. Holly would get totally fixated on an idea and not let it go. Patty and I became fast friends. We had many similar interests: a love of gardening, food, and children that often drove us to distraction.

We would often get together to take Robert and Holly to see movies their contemporaries would have thought babyish. One such outing, after we were seated in the theater, Holly realized she had misplaced her mitten. "Patty I lost my mitten," she said, tapping her mom on the arm. She always called her mom Patty instead of Mom. I don't know why it started, they never got her to change, so Patty just accepted it. "It's okay Holly, we'll find it after the movie," Patty said, since it was already dark in the theater. "I lost my mitten Patty," Holly restated, as though for the first time. "It's okay Hol, we'll find it later." Of course by this time I was starting to laugh. I had often been in the same situation.

Holly didn't care the theater was dark, and the shadowy floor was not giving up a mitten without a fight. Patty was soon down on her hands and knees scrounging the sticky floor while Holly continued her tantrum. Patty and I were both lucky to have thick hair, we joked that we'd both have been bald from tearing our hair out in frustration otherwise.

One summer, my sister Deb introduced us to Keanne Cameron a swim instructor who loved teaching swimming to special needs people. Deb's son Connor who has Autism was involved in the program. Keanne had tremendous enthusiasm and patience. He was teaching a program in a friend's private pool. I would join my sister poolside and think, "I wish Rob were as trim as his cousin Connor." Deb's thoughts probably focused on how verbal Rob was and how she wished her own son was as was able to articulate his ideas and wishes.

By the following winter, Keanne obtained the use of a private school's pool. Parents dropped the kids off at the school and later picked them up. Keanne did this without charging the students. He also coached Special Olympics swimming and got people involved in state meets. One of his students actually went to China for the world games. Keanne impacted many lives and was nominated one year for The Eleven Who Care, a local network news award for high achievers in volunteering.

CHAPTER FIFTEEN

HIGH SCHOOL GROWING PAINS

You would think all the exercising I made Robert do would have produced a slender muscular person. Any normal child who participated in sports at the level Robert did would certainly be healthy and fit. However, PWS doesn't work that way. Despite my best efforts, by sophomore year his weight was 200 pounds. His weight kept him from participating in downhill skiing and horseback riding. This both saddened and scared me.

I started to see more food seeking behaviors now Robert was in high school, because he was able to gain access to food at school. Candy was taken from desks of unsuspecting teachers, or from classmates who didn't notice. I found wrappers in his pant pockets and asked, "Where did you get the candy?" His reply was always, "Oh, my friend gave it to me." We also saw Robert's tantrums increase in both frequency and intensity once ninth grade began.

High school can often be a time of more isolation for special needs people as the distance between them and their peers grows. Other normal kids move further and further away from their parents as they begin driving, getting a job, gaining independence and testing boundaries. Robert, like most special needs children continue to have

113

everything arranged and managed by their parents. Robert would never have thought to get someone's number at school to arrange a get-together, or independently decide to participate in an activity. A solution to the typical high school isolation arrived though The Highland Friendship Club.

Two mothers of children with special needs, Pat Leseman and Rose Fagrelius faced the same problem as I did. Pat's oldest son, attended Cretin Derham, a private Catholic high school. Her son who was popular with the other students, would have lunch with his special needs brother, who attended another school. Private schools do not have the diversity a public school would have. Pat and Rose devised a plan to have adult leaders and student volunteers create social events for challenged teens. Cretin Derham had a volunteer requirement, and the kids were eager to help make an impact. It worked beautifully. Friendship Club was born. It put on retreats, dances, movie nights, yoga, and in the summer months, Adventure Club, which was a summer day program.

Adventure Club was initially run by a special education teacher from St Paul. He took club members on outings all over the city. Garbed in knee socks, pith helmet and walking shorts, his enthusiastic personality set the tone. He also brought extra pith helmets for anyone who would wear them. Now Friendship has a board and expanded opportunities. It fills a nitch in our children's socialization many parents had longed for.

When I spoke with Pat about how she was able to cope with her son's challenges, she told me she liked to play tennis as a way to have time for herself. She realized how easily your life can be consumed by your child's medical needs, and it took her many years to realize, as she states "Life begins when you stop trying to fix the problems."

When Robert was 15 he was legally able to apply for a driver's permit. What a scary thought it was. We watched him motor around on his motorized trike without sideswiping cars, driving seemed like a very dangerous venture. Robert was very excited about driving. He was so focused on getting his permit I wasn't sure how to handle the situation. Someone mentioned Courage Center had a driving assessment program for both special needs and aging adults. This was the answer because it would give Robert an honest evaluation of his driving and the best part was the judgment wasn't coming from Carey or me.

We called and scheduled an appointment. On the day of the test, Robert and I arrived at Courage Center and I watched as Robert and the instructor went to a car while I waited for the driving test to be administered. After the driving assessment the instructor told Robert, "I am so sorry you are not able to drive. Your depth perception and motor skills make it unsafe." Of course I'd prepared myself for this; I knew he wouldn't be able to drive. So, I wasn't surprised a huge meltdown was the immediate result. "The reason I failed the test is the man's fault! He kept telling me to do the wrong thing!" Robert screamed. I hustled him out of the office, his tears and screams echoing down the hall. It was impossible to reason with him. Most people take the freedom to drive a car and be independent for granted. My heart was heavy. Robert would be dependent on others to drive him places, or on public transportation for the rest of his life.

Amid all the tantrums and unmet milestones for Robert this year, love brought us a wonderful gift. At age twenty-one, Cara married Justin and soon had a beautiful baby boy, Rory. Of course we were concerned they were marrying so young. Justin and Cara couldn't have been more different. Justin made Cara laugh unlike no one else. We were over the moon with Rory, he brought us such joy. I always tell people grandchildren are the reward for raising your own children. You finally know how fast they grow so you cherish every moment.

Cath and I would babysit marveling at Rory's beautiful baby skin. We would change his diaper and then try to get his kicking legs back into the adorable baby jeans Cara had put on him. We would just manage to get one leg in while he kicked the other off. We were hysterical with laughter, loving every minute of our time with our new grandbaby.

Eleven months later Kelly married Rob, (Yes, we had another Robert joining the family!) and moved into a home in St. Paul. Steve finished college and got a job working in the mental health unit of Fairview Riverside Medical Center.

During his junior year Robert surprised us by trying out for the Speech Team. Keely, a friend from elementary school, helped and encouraged him. After he made the team, Keely always made sure he had a ride to the meets. Knowing he was getting picked up by a friend, Robert, wearing a suit and tie, got ready for the meet and was out the door in record time. This definitely made Carey and I feel positive about his future. This was the first thing he'd done that was not adaptive; he was competing with normal students. He had sought it out himself. Keely was the team captain and made sure everyone was involved in social events, including Robert.

Senior year Robert lettered in Speech. We were so proud; our family knew it was an amazing accomplishment. We bought a letter jacket so Robert could display his achievement. Keely said, "They didn't just give Robert a letter, He really had to earn it." She was such a wonderful friend and helped to make speech team a reality for Robert.

Graduation day was fast approaching. We were all excited for this momentous occasion, we had to start thinking about the future. Minnesota allows special needs students to continue their schooling free until the age of twenty-one. So I sat down with all of Robert's service providers in the spring to talk about future plans. The Dakota County Vocational College (DCTC) had a program in place for students with special needs. Life skills along with work opportunities were part of the curriculum. It sounded like a wonderful program to Carey and me, when we told Robert about the program he lost all control. "I am going to college! You are not sending me to a vocational school! I won't go there! This is all your fault Mom. I won't go to that school!" These phrases were screamed at the service providers and me over and over because Robert was part of the meeting. It was the worst school meeting imaginable, and we left the school with the tantrum still in full swing.

I think this was the first time Robert really had to face his limitations. He never thought of himself as less than before. The Pokémon and the Power Ranger characters he idolized could do anything if they didn't give up, he believed this about himself too. Special needs children get accolades, medals, and awards for just participating in Special Olympics. I believe they gave Robert an unrealistic view of his abilities. The end of senior year was filled with tantrums and angry accusations about what Robert's future had in store.

Robert graduates from Sibley High School

CHAPTER SEVENTEEN

THE LONG HOT SUMMER AFTER GRADATION

The summer following graduation was hard on everyone. Robert had a graduation open house and received several gifts of cash just like all graduating seniors. However, soon his gifts were everywhere. The bills were stuffed in Robert's pockets every time he left the house, falling out in random rooms, at his family members' homes, on the street, in cars, everywhere. He placed the coins in a jar and counted them constantly, the rattling often continuing through the night. Looking back now we realize it was foolish to allow him to manage his gift money, but, at the time there was so much conflict about other things it seemed cruel to take away his gifts. In Robert's mind, putting the money into a savings account would have been the same as just taking it from him. Like a small child, he wouldn't have been able to accept our taking charge of his gift money.

Set to start at DCTC in the fall, Robert was going to work at Tree Trust for the summer. Tree Trust is an outdoor environmental program located at the Dodge Nature Center near our home. The program taught at-risk teens and special needs children how to work outdoors. Robert went for four hours each day. There the staff showed him and his workmates to how to remove invasive plants like buckthorn, how to plant trees, and work on retaining walls. Since this was job training, they also taught money management. At the time I was hopeful Robert might one day live independently and this could be helpful. His management of graduation gifts certainly demonstrated help would be necessary. When I learned more about the syndrome, I discovered most people with PWS cannot be trusted to manage their own finances. It could cause possible overspending on food or extreme anxiety. The program did give me time to get catering work done and also some personal time to recharge. Robert also felt a sense of accomplishment in completed projects.

Social Security also set up an assessment to determine Robert's eligibility for SSI. This is the benefit people receive if they are unable to earn enough to take care of themselves. Since Robert was 18, he was interviewed and assessed independently even though he had PWS. This meant I was not part of the assessment nor was my husband, or any of Robert's previous service workers. Initially, I didn't necessarily think this was an issue because they had his diagnosis and could access school records and other information. During the assessment, Robert told the psychologist in charge of his assessment, he was working in landscaping. Instead of looking into Tree Trust or verifying the information, this trained evaluator believed Robert, and took what he said at face value. Because of this, Robert was initially denied SSI.

We hired an attorney and had to jump through all kinds of hoops to try to attain benefits for Robert. All of the written doctor's statements were ignored when reviewed by Social Security. I talked to our congresswoman and everyone I could think of trying to find help. It seemed like the bureaucracy in place was just trying to get me to go away. The funding we received from Dakota County ended at age 18 so now we now had to pay for all of Robert's programs and extra medical costs. Not to mention the efforts to get Robert's SSI payments were costly and frustrating. Carey has a strong career, and both Cara and Robert received a small inheritance from Carey's parents when they passed away. If we hadn't had that, I don't know how we would have been able to afford all of Robert's needs. Even with the blessings we had, it was a stressful time trying to make ends meet. It took three years of working through the bureaucratic nightmare before we would be able to get him the benefits he deserved.

Summer was ending and the plan for Robert's further education was beginning. He would be bussed to DCTC. He was still furious because he felt he should have been attending "real college" and so he became extremely uncooperative. I would wake each morning at five and a two-hour battle would commence to get Rob on the bus. It was a dreadful time for us all. My life consisted of screaming at my defiant son who was becoming more and more disconnected with reality.

There were times when Robert seemed completely lost in fantasy. He came home one day and announced "I'm getting married today." Thinking it was a joke I said, "Who are you marrying?" to which he calmly replied, "Oh, Rachel from high school." He then proceeded to go to his room, put on his suit and walk back out the front door. I was shocked by this series of events and as he walked out of the house I snapped to my senses, calling after him, "You're not getting married! Get back in the house!" It was a struggle to get him back into the house and redirected.

He also began roaming the house at night. One night he took his massive collection of DVDs off the shelves and piled them on the floor. Several times I woke about three in the morning to find him standing by my bed. Startled, I'd ask him what he was doing out of bed. He calmly replied, "I'm going out to the bus." Still half asleep and completely shaken by his actions I'd say, "It's only three in the morning Robert. The bus doesn't come for another four hours. Go back to bed!" Initially, this would get him back to his bed.

Because everyone always loves to hold parties at the holidays, the following December brought its usual overload of catering work for me. Both Cara and Kelly also worked with me. They had been my assistants from a very young age and since parties typically occur in the evening and on weekends, they continued to work for me, although they both had real jobs.

Just before Christmas I catered a huge party, one I'd spent many days prepping for. I'd already gone to the party with my car loaded down with food to finish prepping and start cooking, while Cara and Kelly were still back at the house packing up the rest of the food. Robert was also home. Although I was used to his increasing bouts of fantasy and being fully immersed in his imaginary world, Cara and Kelly were not. They had heard me talk about them they had yet witness one of these episodes.

That was about to change. Cara was upstairs in the kitchen in our split-level home while Kelly was running between the kitchen and garage packing the car. During a run Kelly overheard Robert talk about going through the portal to see his other family. She was shaken by his erratic behavior and what he was saying, and quietly, without Rob realizing it, called to Cara. They both stood in the entryway listening to Robert make intricate plans for his escape. They were very scared and saw this as a definite indication of mental illness. Cara immediately called Carey while Kelly called her mom. Cath came over right away since Cara and Kelly still needed to get to the catering party. Cath agreed with their recommendation. Carey bring Robert to the mental health emergency room. Cath accompanied both Carey and Robert to the hospital.

When Robert was first admitted to the emergency room and started to speak with the doctor, Cath said he was lucid and seemed fine, cordial and happy to answer the doctor's questions. At one point something the doctor said snapped him back into his imaginary world. Then he became very involved in describing his plans for escaping this world and going through the portal. These statements were enough to get him admitted for a psychiatric evaluation. Looking back, I realize Carey and I had both been in denial about Robert's changing mental condition. We both thought his behavior was temporary, a reaction to change, and after he adjusted to his new "normal" he would stop slipping into his imaginary world. It took Cara and Kelly witnessing his actions and demanding we do something caused us to act. Although I was sure they were overreacting when they got to the party and told me what had happened, I couldn't have been more wrong.

Fairview Riverside, has a large psychiatric unit and mental health emergency room on their Riverside campus. This was Robert's home for several weeks following the emergency room incident. As a patient, Robert was allowed visitors for one hour, every evening at six. Robert's condition seemed to worsen overnight. He was disconnected from reality, mumbling to himself, and paying no attention to what was said to him. The medication he received had no impact on his behavior or the delusions. We felt like we had lost our son. It was terrifying.

Mental illness still carries a stigma. Generally, people don't understand it and are afraid of it. Carey and I visited almost every night of our Robert's month long stay. Sadly, we noticed t many patients had no visitors at all. During those first few nights, we listened to him mumble about Zordon, a Power Rangers character he watched on TV. We brought him lattes—his favorite treat. One night we brought a muffin, which he began eating without removing the paper wrapper. "Robert what are you doing?" I barked at him, completely shocked by his behavior. Two weeks later there was still no improvement. By the end of the month things had stabilized, it certainly wasn't the end of his mental health problems, those will be ongoing for the rest of his life.

The hospital had also placed no limits on Robert's calories other than giving him low fat dressing on a salad. He also scavenged food from other patients. During his one-month hospitalization, he gained 25 to 30 pounds. I was furious and spoke to staff and doctors. Nothing was done to control food intake.

Cath joined me one night for a visit, before I got out of the car she looked at me and said "I think you should look for a place for Robert to live when he gets out of the hospital. I don't think you are going to be able to take care of him." I was shocked. This was something we haven't even considered. Of course he would come home, I'd thought, because he'd get better and back to normal when he got out. It took a while, Carey and I soon realized Cath was right.

The hospital social worker and Robert's county social worker were no help. They felt it would be quite difficult to find a place for Robert when he was released. Neither offered any assistance; we were on our own. I was surprised and disappointed. Wasn't that their job? There are often times when people you depend on to help you let you down. The only thing to do is keep networking to find answers, so we focused on finding the answer ourselves. Cath suggested some places she knew about from her many years in nursing case management. Cara made it her mission to help us and searched the internet ceaselessly.

One day Cara found a group home for people with PWS called Stepping Out. Ironically, I'd spoken to Carolyn Jones, our nurse from Gillette Hospital, the same day and she also suggested Stepping Out. We were hopeful this could be the answer to our prayers and called them immediately.

We were extremely fortunate, Stepping Out had an opening for another client, or consumer, as they are called in the group home world. Two days later Cara and I met with Bonny Bates, the owner of the Stepping Out, and her staff. Cara had worked as a personal care attendant in several group homes. It was great to have her assistance, as she knew what questions to ask, and what signs to look for in the house. Everything looked great. However, Robert still had no income because SSI had continued to deny benefits. Bonnie answered our prayers in this situation as well. She assured us she would be able to get funding from Dakota County. She'd seen this before and had overcome these hurdles in the past.

Bonnie's Story

Bonnie won my heart immediately. She had a daughter, Laurie, who had PWS. She was several years older than Robert and had grown up when very little was known about the syndrome. Laurie had not been diagnosed until age 28. I could only imagine how frustrating and difficult it must have been.

Bonnie and her daughter had been living in Colorado when Laurie was diagnosed, and moved to Minnesota where research was being done. There Bonnie began to educate herself about the syndrome. Using her new insights and her master's degree in psychology, Bonnie designed the group home to accommodate only people who had PWS. She had worked with Marty McGraw to design group homes in the western suburbs of Minneapolis called AME, and then took this model to open her own group home in Hastings.

She believed Robert's breakdown was just another part of PWS. I was surprised. No one at the hospital had even suggested this mental break was connected to PWS. Bonnie felt that if Robert lived at Stepping Out, and worked her program in conjunction with his doctors' care, he would start to heal.

I have often felt God's presence in my life. God has helped me though times of deep despair by sending me people like Bonnie. In a week's time she found funding and had the paperwork in place for Robert to enter Stepping Out. Understanding PWS and having many transitions under her belt over the years, Bonnie suggested we hold a party at the house with staff and Robert's house mates so Robert could "check it out." The party was a success. Robert agreed to live at Stepping Out. We couldn't have been happier, having this positive transition reinforced right out of the gate. We'd found a loving place and, hopefully, the answer to Robert's needs.

Kelly and Carey moved all of Robert's belonging to his new home one cold January day. Stepping Out provided

Robert's bed and dresser, because it would have been difficult to move big furniture in the cold. Kelly arranged everything in his newly painted room. She was always the organizer and there when needed, for which I'm very thankful. Setting up a room for Robert alone would not have been easy for Carey.

Bonnie coordinated Robert's discharge from the hospital. Relinquishing responsibility lifted our spirits, as not bringing him home was heart wrenching. We were still trying to cope with this major and unexpected change. Aside from his hospital stays, this would be the first time in nineteen years we would not be supervising Robert's daily care.

CHAPTER EIGHTEEN

STEPPING OUT SUCCESS STORIES

Stepping Out is located in Hastings, about a 25-minute drive from our home. It consists of several family homes, all close together, converted into small apartments. Each person has their own room, while a communal dining and TV room is shared by two or three people. A gym with weights, stationary bikes, treadmills and stretching area, is shared by all.

The task of changing the habits of a lifetime is a challenge for each new individual that joins Stepping Out. Now it was Robert's turn. His whole life was about to change. Robert would now be allowed to consume only 1,500 calories on a daily basis. Exercise was encouraged and rewarded. Compliance and good behavior was rewarded. All rewards were food, the exact opposite of our home. As a result, Robert shed one hundred pounds in a year.

All of the people living at Stepping Out had once been morbidly obese. Some had carried as much as 450 pounds on their small frames and needed walkers and wheelchairs to get around. They would all lose the weight they carried and begin a lifelong journey of keeping it off.

I spoke to an older female with PWS living in a group home specifically for people with the syndrome. She had lived in a more traditional group home with residents of assorted disabilities. "They were mean and threw things at me," she said. No one paid attention to her diet and when she finally tipped the scales at 450 pounds, she had to go to the hospital. Her doctor found Stepping Out. He told her, "I am not going to send you back to die." She is very happy living at the group home, and now weighs about 135 pounds. This story illustrates how much has changed in twenty years. The ease of diagnose has meant people with the syndrome are able to have access to care. The medical community is better able to refer patients to people that can help.

The program Bonnie designed for the group home uses the syndrome to beat the syndrome. There is no access to food or money, both are locked up. This decreases anxiety since there is no opportunity to steal food. Three meals and snacks are provided each day at an exact time, so there is also lessened anxiety because everyone knows exactly when the next meal is coming. Exercising is done at least once a day, more often twice daily. Active recreation hobbies and crafts are also encouraged. Working is also encouraged, there must be no access to food. Residents can earn treats (food rewards) for meeting exercise goals or behavior goals, which is highly motivating for them.

Talk about a tough program! Many of my friends have asked to live there to get their own weight under control! It took a long time for me to process all this. Carey has always been better at detaching. At first, I couldn't understand how taking Robert out for a coffee or dinner sabotaged his success. At Stepping Out, he had to work to earn his food rewards in the program. If I took him out there was no incentive for him to work. I had to learn new habits as well.

Robert exploited the guilt I felt placing him in a group home. He would call and cry about how much he hated it there. He knew all the things to say to me to increase my guilt. He'd tell me he missed me, or ask why wouldn't I come down and see him. He knew he could talk me into a treat, which sabotaged his program at Stepping Out. And for a long time I allowed it. It was really hard for me to understand. I figured he was already eating such a small number of calories and working out so much, what was the harm in buying him a latte or a treat when we were together. Looking back, my own mental state was not very healthy, I was exhausted and depressed after all the crises we had endured. I hadn't yet been able to sort everything out.

Cath suggested I join her family on a trip to Hawaii. It was the first extended vacation I had taken away from Robert since he was a baby. I slept ten hours a night and napped during the day. There was nothing I had to do but enjoy paradise. It restored my spirit. When I returned home I realized my life had changed. I told friends it seemed as though I was still on vacation. The days of driving Robert to doctor appointments, sports, social activities, and school were over. I was able to work without thinking about his care. Carey and I were able to travel. We both were free to eat what we wanted when we wanted. Our son was by no means well, still he was in capable hands.

There were still school meetings to attend, finalizing the SSI benefits and finding a medication to help with Robert's delusions. While he was hospitalized the physiatrist prescribed one drug on top of another to cure his hallucinations. By the time he was finally discharged his list of medications was staggering. I started to wonder if any of them were helping. A friend from church who is a psychiatric nurse told me once, "It's a crap shoot. They pile on medications until something works." After hospitalization the psychiatrist will try to reduce the number of drugs the patient is taking. However, this has to be done slowly, because of side effects.

People who have the neurological problems associated with PWS are often subject to side effects. Robert was no exception. Many of his drugs have a side effect called tardive dyskinesia. This means the drug will cause uncontrolled facial ticks, lip licking, or other body movements often become permanent. It is painful to witness the medication's effects on your child; their pupils are dilated, their speech is slowed, their attention limited, and they have no zest for life. Stepping Out monitored this and reported back to the psychiatrist. They have a test called the Moses Discus. It determines if the movement is part of the medication or part of the syndrome.

Daniel and Serena's Story

Both Daniel and Serena's parents feel the same as I do about medications. They are frustrated the psychotropic medications have so many side effects. "Some medications can also increase hunger, yet are given to PWS patients," Serena's mom, a pharmacist, said. Both parents just want the person they love back.

I understand the desire so well. I had continued to go to all of Robert's psychiatrist's appointments. I knew him best and wanted him to be well. I was often frustrated and impatient. "Do you know he sleeps for most of the day in school?" I would ask. "Oh, yes, sometimes that's a side effect," would be the reply. "Well, not just sometimes, it's every day!" I'd say. It was difficult to see Robert totally snowed by psychotropic drugs. It seemed so unfair. I had pushed and pushed to see our son succeed. Now all the hard work was down the drain. I wondered if it would be this way forever. He barely communicated or interacted with the real world, He would mumble softly to his imaginary family. I told him how sad this made me. Robert replied, "I'm sorry, my other mom and 2,000 brothers and sisters need me more." It was certainly a shocking statement for me to hear. It did help me realize it was time for me to get some help for myself.

Constance's Story

Constance had been our family counselor at Gillette for many years. She had a private practice in Minneapolis. She understood all the issues which special needs parents have.

I was able to talk about the losses in my life and she helped me work though them.

Constance said at some point I was going to have to be able to disengage from my over involvement in Robert's life. When I mentioned this to Carey, he gleefully said "You see, I was right all along, disengaging is the best way to live. You don't have to get so involved in other peoples' lives. It's so much easier my way!" He was joking, of course, Carey also felt a profound sadness over our son's condition. Humor was just his favorite way of dealing with the pressures.

Talking to Constance helped me to see myself clearly. I was a determined person who wanted quick results. I had baggage from my parents' alcohol abuse and my own abuse issues I'd never dealt with.

For years I felt Cara had no right to the pain she expressed when she acted out. She had two parents who loved her and gave her plenty of attention. Cara felt "Robert got away with everything and was able to manipulate me into giving him what he wanted." It seemed to me having two sober parents should be enough.

Each of us process situations differently. The resentments Cara felt were hard for her to express, and hard for me to hear. Amanda, Robert's current PCA said, "People with PWS amaze me with their brilliance at getting what they want. They manipulate the staff and remember everything to their advantage." In my defense I tried to always be fair, what mother wins against those odds?

Constance helped me process the losses I had in my life, and to accept "my world as it was, not what I wished it was." I'd done the best I could do for both of my children. Cara was on her own journey. I wish I could have given Cara more of what she needed.

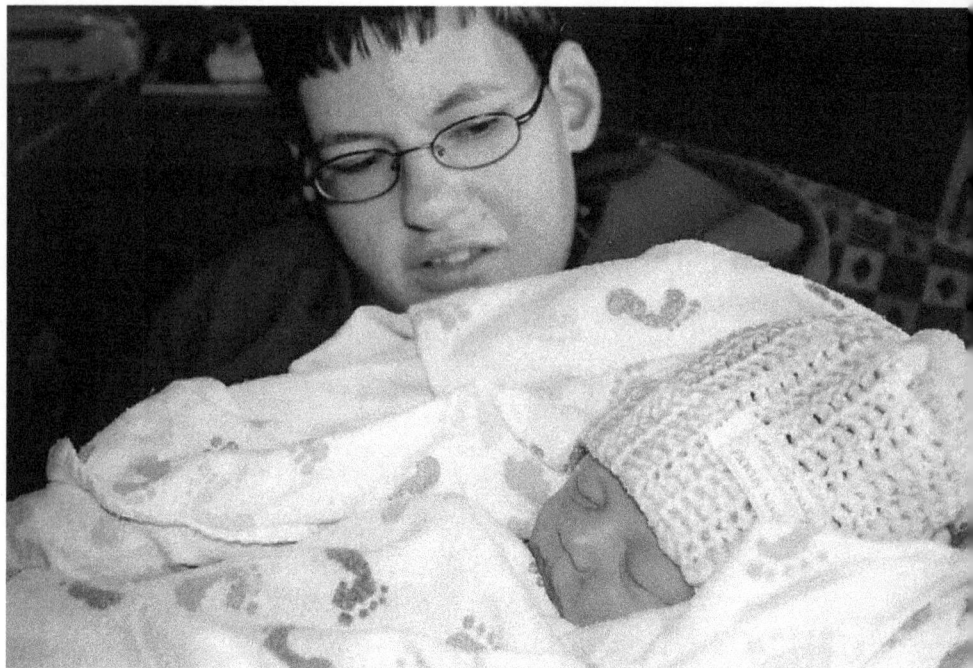

ROBERT WITH NEPHEW RORY

CHAPTER NINETEEN

CELEBRATIONS

The weight was melting off Robert's body with his low calorie diet and exercise program. The staff was frustrated by his lack of consistency. He very seldom earned the rewards offered for doing his exercise program in a timely manner. It would take him years to achieve rewards on a regular basis.

Part of the reason for this was all the medication he was on sapped his energy. Another reason was my inability to let the program work. When visiting I often took Robert to coffee. I had yet to see how giving him the small treat made him less motivated to work for his rewards.

The staff also thought he might be getting extra food somewhere. He would go down five pounds, up four pounds then down seven pounds in a two-week period. Eventually the staff found this was normal for him. I thought about all my dieting failures, I would always give up because the scale showed no change.

Eventually 100 pounds were gone from Robert's frame. His goal weight was 160 pounds. His accomplishment was celebrated by all the staff and housemates. Stepping Out celebrates birthdays, holidays, even Mondays. They have a Monday evening event called Picnic in the Park during the summer months where the residents and staff go to a local park for a barbeque and games after dinner. The group often voted to play kick ball. Playing this simple game with a group of friends was something Robert had never experienced. The rules were modified, such as no throwing a ball to tag someone, it was highly competitive and fun. One of the items on my regret list had been erased.

CHAPTER TWENTY

WORKING THROUGH PSYCHOSIS WITH PWS

Seventy-five percent of people with PWS have a chromosome deletion from the father. The other twenty-five percent have what is called a maternal uniparental disomy from the mother which is a factor of the mother's age.

Theresa's Story

Theresa, another of Bonny's daughters, and who now runs Stepping Out, helped to educate me about this. She mentioned people with the maternal uniparental disomy have a higher incidence of mental illness. She thought Robert fit in this category because he had some of the other characteristics.

The genetic testing, we had done at Gillette had not indicated if Robert had uniparental disomy (UPD). Research shows those PWS patients with psychoses were usually UPD. They had active and extroverted behaviors in their youth, while those with mood disorders were generally more introverted and less active in childhood.

I understand the parents of younger children with PWS being scared to death reading about the problems their child may face in later life. This was one of the reasons I never anticipated the future, it was a scary place. This is our family's journey. If you are a parent of a child with PWS your journey will not be the same as mine, especially considering the medical advances.

Dr. Anislie, the endocrinologist who treated Robert at Gillette, spoke to me of parents of newly diagnosed PWS children. He said they come to him having searched the internet with all kinds of questions about the future. He says, "I try to focus on present issues. Some of the parents' concerns may or may not be a problem for them in the future." We can become overwhelmed when we try to handle tomorrow's problems today.

There are many common traits with PWS, people with PWS may or may not be affected by them. They may have a problem with something like stubbornness, yet not all the time. One of the behaviors common with PWS is skin and rectal picking. This was a huge concern with Robert. He was not able to go to the bathroom alone, especially at night. Otherwise, there would be spots of blood on his underwear and sheets in the morning.

I asked Theresa why this happens. She said with low muscle tone, bowel movements can be difficult so rectal picking becomes a helpful, though inappropriate, way to eliminate. The shame most people would feel about rectal picking is not evident in most of the residents. They freely talk about it, which shocked me, Bonny simply states, "They have no ick factor." However, Robert and the other residents do understand this is inappropriate behavior. When I asked him about how many times it happens in a week he minimizes the problem. He doesn't like to discuss it, or the occasional bed wetting which has occurred since he has been taking so many medications. He generally responds, "Oh it happened once this week." He also uses this technique to minimize other things he doesn't want to talk about. Ultimately, the staff strategized on how to break him of nighttime picking. Someone suggesting a wrestling singlet be worn over Depends, for limiting access at night. It has been somewhat successful.

The psychosis plaguing Robert was ongoing. During one acute episode Robert was clearly in distress about something, and seemed unable to speak. We brought him to the ER at St. Joseph's Hospital in St Paul. He spent most of the day there mouthing words silently. Finally, he began speaking coherently in the evening. Bonnie and I discussed getting Robert admitted to the Children's Institute of Pittsburgh Their focus was holistic including diet, exercise, and mental health. I strongly believed they could help cure our son's mental illness.

Another young man at Stepping Out named Daniel had been admitted there. Medical assistance had approved his care, so I contacted the Institute for more information. They agreed Robert could benefit from treatment at the Institute.

The Institute treats both adults and children with PWS, and have individualized psychiatric and behavioral treatments. Unlike general psychiatric units, they have absolute food control. The hospital has a whole team of doctors and therapists who communicate with each other about patients. This team approach is important to create the whole picture of the patient. Ninety-five percent of patients do not return to the hospital for at least nine months.

However, medical assistance would not agree to pay for Robert's treatment at the institute. Their opinion was we had not yet tried all the options Minnesota had to offer. I would encourage people to seek help at the Institute before the patient goes on medical assistance.

Eventually we went back to Gillette for psychiatric care. We felt with the PWS clinic there, the rest of the staff would be familiar with the syndrome. Gillette is a children's hospital; it continues to treat their patients into adulthood. We began seeing Dr. W., a psychiatrist on staff. She continued to titrate Robert's medications, slowly reducing dosages. We'd been seeing her for about six months when I asked if she would be willing to consult with The Pittsburg Institute because Robert hadn't improved much. She stared at me and calmly responded, "What can I say, other than Robert's mother is impatient for him to be well." I stared at her, astounded by what I perceived as her dismissive attitude. I couldn't understand why she wouldn't want to at least inquire if there was something else she could try. This was the last time we met with her.

The education Robert received after high school was mostly wasted. The teachers and staff were top notch. Robert was either catatonic from so many drugs, or highly delusional, so hardly participated. I was hopeful he could learn some type of computer technology to qualify him for employment opportunities, as the typing and game playing skills Robert had in high school were quite good. Sadly, he had little or no interest in learning much of anything. Keeping awake was his biggest challenge, and after three years of attending DCTC, Robert graduated. We were sad to see his school career end so negatively. However, Theresa assured me other Stepping Out residents took college classes and there were other opportunities available.

Karl, Rob's current PCA, was full of suggestions. Karl was a film study buff. He had made the Stepping Out video, A Clear Choice. The video documented the group home's programs, focusing on their Run Club, food rewards, staff education, and personal stories of success. What a delightful person. Karl was full of enthusiasm for helping Robert attain his goals.

Karl worked with Robert to write scripts for movies. He directed two plays the group home performed as well. One centered around our dog Charley. Everyone loved Charley. The residents performed the plays for family and a local nursing home. Directing plays was not in Karl's job description, like all the staff, he went above and beyond what he was paid to do.

Eventually Karl moved on to continue his career in film. Most of the people who do PCA jobs are just starting their working lives. They finish school, most work part time, and begin careers. Some of the staff stay for long periods of time, and there are many tearful goodbyes. Saying goodbye is a hard reality for all the residents, as they spend so much time with these people. The staff members have better social skills than most people and become supportive friends of the residents. It takes a lot of motor planning to have a conversation. "Normal" friendships are built by exchanging information on mutual interests. We say "Hello how are you?" After the person replies, we ask about them and what are they involved in at the time. Often people with special needs have social anxiety and do not excel at thinking of others. Their conversations revolve around what "they" are interested in at the moment. It takes someone with special gifts to become friends with someone who has special needs and is not looking for a mutual exchange, where there will be equal give and take.

CHAPTER TWENTY-ONE

FINALLY GETTING SSI

We worked the system for two years to get Robert's SSI benefits. He was certainly disabled. We continued to get letters from Social Security which said they would not be giving him benefits. It took another year for us to obtain benefits. Robert had his housing and food paid for, no other money.

We finally got a court date. I was not allowed in the court room because I was going to testify. Waiting in the hall I strained to hear what was going on. Robert began screaming "I have an IQ of more than 70, you fucking shrink. I don't have Prader-Willi, my Doctor told me there was a mistake!" On and on he ranted, while I was out in the hall, helpless to make a difference, and wondering why no one was stopping his behavior.

"He got his benefits!" said our lawyer, while exiting the courtroom. "Thank God! Why did the judge let him go on for so long?" I inquired. Our lawyer responded off-hand, "Oh, when people have waited so long for a court date the judge likes to just let them speak." I thought this was ridiculous, still I was happy his SSI issue was finally resolved, However, Robert repeated, "I do not have Prader-Willi" all the way home.

We eventually received payments for the years Social Security had denied them. They initially came in $2,000.00 increments because if you have over $2,000.00 you are ineligible to receive benefits. Our first check was for $1,900.00. A year later we received a check for $10,000.00. You would think this would be fantastic, yet it felt like just another way for SSI to deny Robert benefits if we didn't spend all the money.

We saw a lawyer and created a Special Needs Trust. They are very complicated yet necessary if the person has income exceeding two thousand dollars. You can only spend the money on specific things for the person's needs, like programs or sports equipment. You have to be able to document everything you purchase, and make sure you stay within the guidelines. It's very tricky and after two years of administering the trust I'm embarrassed to say I unintentionally broke the trust. SSI immediately responded. I was able to work through a payment plan so Robert didn't lose SSI completely. I bring it up as a warning. If you create something similar, be very clear on the parameters and don't get lazy or forget them.

If you are struggling to get SSI, it's important to know PWS is not on the list of SSI impairments. The PWS Association of Minnesota has prepared materials to help people with the syndrome gain benefits. They are accessible on their website. You can use the forms they have created in your initial application. Of course, this does not guarantee benefits.

Chapter Twenty-Two

Getting Our Son Back

Bonnie continued her quest to find a psychiatrist sympathetic to the needs of her group home residents. Her research led her to Diane, CPN. She had a private practice in Brooklyn Park, an hour drive from Hastings.

I attended the first meeting with Diane. Robert was totally delusional. At the intake interview Robert gave nonsensical answers. His delusions were so intense; he often wouldn't even respond. The frustration you feel as a parent witnessing this type of behavior is overwhelming. I wanted to shake Robert and say "answer her!" I was the only person in the room who knew the darling boy Robert had been.

Diane was quietly reassuring, telling me "Yes, of course, I would be willing to contact The Pittsburg Institute." She also wanted to try the old drug Haldol. She'd had good success using it in small doses. We agreed to the new medication change. We would meet with Diane every three months for medication checks and for counseling sessions every month.

Robert began to slowly let go of his delusions. The new medication Diane prescribed worked. It was hard to trust another miracle; we had tried so many options I kept waiting for the other shoe to drop. Finally, we accepted we had our son back from his alternate universe. It had been a long five years. The family was all so grateful.

Several years later I asked Diane why she thought of trying Haldol. She stated, "I noted Robert hadn't been on Haldol in the past. When I first saw Robert I didn't see someone with PWS. I saw someone who was hallucinating, he looked miserable and tortured. Haldol doesn't work for everyone I'm so glad it works well for Robert."

We soon saw improvement in the workout and reward program at Stepping Out too. Weight had become a non-issue, Robert regularly met the requirement. His exercise goals had remained elusive. Either he quit before finishing, had a tantrum, or just decided not to work out. The staff couldn't make him do anything, they could only encourage. Now he was doing so well with his medication, he sometimes earned dinner out on Saturday night, or a Dairy Queen a couple times a month.

The mumbling talk to his imaginary family completely stopped. We now had conversations at coffee about our family life. I once asked "Do you still think about your other family?" to which Robert replied, "No not really, they kind of went away." I wasn't sure what to say, so I asked if it made him sad not to think about them. His answer was simply, "no." I certainly did not miss being left out of his conversations, sitting there feeling sad while he smiled at things only he heard.

The effects of mental illness on a family can be catastrophic. Carey and I believe we would probably have gone bankrupt if Robert hadn't been cared for by Stepping Out. We knew at Stepping Out, someone would give him his medication, make sure he ate, brushed his teeth, put on deodorant, and get him off to work.

A person as mentally ill as Robert, cannot be left alone. We would have had to pay home health aides to care for him. Twenty-five to thirty hours of care a month could be paid for from his Social Security benefits, we would have to continue to pay for all his other expenses. Because he lived independently from his family in a group home the state paid for Medical Assistance and some living expenses. Robert's hospitalization had been for three weeks. Imagine negotiating with your insurance company for more mental health coverage.

People with family members who are just mentally ill, struggle to keep it all together. They care for someone who often doesn't like the effect of the drugs they are taking, so they stop. Erratic behavior begins and often ends with a crisis, followed by hospitalization. Eventually it can become too much and the family gives up on the person. We witnessed this at the Fairview Riverside Psychiatric ward. Visitors are allowed one hour a day, from six p.m. to seven. Often only one or two family members were visiting with the twelve patients.

I have volunteered for one organization called People Inc. The organization works to remove the stigma of mental illness. They have small houses where people with mental illness can stay while in crisis. They can avoid hospitalization and the administration of drugs, which may or may not help. People Inc. provides art therapy classes, focusing on painting, sculpture and writing. An art show called Artibility is staged each year showcasing the art and draws a large crowd, helping people see mental illness.

National Awareness of Mental Illness (NAMI) works on mental illness education. Their website offers several short videos on mental health problems and some solutions. The president of the organization speaks about treating others with kindness and compassion. It initially sounds like a simplistic solution. NAMI feels if people with mental illness are treated with kindness and compassion they are more likely to seek out help when they need it.

With the help of several residents, Bonnie Bates planned and staged an in-service with the police in Hastings for this reason. Police are called when a person living in the group home cannot be controlled by the staff. "Does it help for us to ask you what is bothering you when you are in meltdown mode?" Sergeant Hanson asked. Jory, a staff person replied "No, it just gets the resident more worked up. A better plan is distraction. For example, did you see my new radio?" Laurie, one of the residents, said "Just be nice." Daniel was worried about being tasered. The in-service was a success and helped the officers better understand what to expect when they are called upon for assistance, more importantly, it helped the residents to feel less anxious.

Alicia's Story

Four years after Robert joined Stepping Out, Alicia, his former schoolmate from middle school, joined the program. Her weight had ballooned to almost 375 pounds. She needed a walker to navigate the world.

Alicia was able to shed about 200 pounds in two years' time. She no longer needs a walker and participates in 5K races. She always seems to be smiling. The two former schoolmates continue to argue about who will sit in the front seat of the car and who will get to be first.

Robert's daily routine involves a workout in the morning before work. He is now employed by East Suburban Resources (ESR). This program gets jobs for people in the community with disabilities. There are several of these programs in the Twin Cities area. Some of the jobs are assembly work. ESR has promoted Robert to a cleaning crew of which he is extremely proud.

Amanda's Story

"The staff at the group home are phenomenal." Amanda, who works as a Care Coordinator and a trainer of new staff spoke about her experience. She told of her admiration of how hard the residents work to fight the syndrome. She is a witness to the despair they can feel when the syndrome takes a front seat— missing a reward or becoming frustrated by a rule.

Parents can have a hard time adjusting to the program, especially if the family is close knit. It can be hard for family members to understand the rules in place. When they see the positive results the program produces they usually get on board. Amanda says the hardest part of her job is being the bad guy. She finds being respectful, giving the residents choices, and helping them problem solve works best.

I asked Robert recently what is the hardest part of having PWS? He said "I think about stealing food all the time." I was surprised and said back, "you never steal food," to which he replied, "I know, but I think about it all the time."

COFFEE TIME

CHAPTER TWENTY-THREE

FINDING BALANCE IN THE END

Theresa's Story

Theresa put together a presentation featuring Stepping Out about their behavior program, which she presented at the National PWS conference in Florida in the fall of 2015. Many of the parents she spoke to were impressed with the program. They were frustrated a similar facility was unavailable in their area. Theresa's response was, "Start your own group home. We have the model; you don't have to reinvent the wheel."

Medical research on PWS continues. Doctor Anislie said "The hard thing about a rare syndrome is, it is difficult to get a group together for a study." Studies are being done by physicians in the field, looking at different medications for different needs. The Children's Institute of Pittsburg offers many clinical trials to get the answers they need for the treatment of the syndrome. They offer care for both children and adults with PWS. They offer individualized psychiatric and behavioral treatment. The hospitalization stay is usually sixty days. Most individuals lose an average of fifty-six pounds during their stay, as well as building cardio endurance.

The Institute also offers consulting services; referral and educational training models they will send to schools' residential facilities, or professional organizations. This organization will gladly share information which can be life changing for people unable to afford treatment.

The hospital's web site offers articles written about people with PWS. Kim Tingley, an author for the New York Times Magazine, wrote a story in 2015 about a young man named Jeremy Girard, who died from complications of the syndrome.

The story relates Jeremy never exhibited many food seeking behaviors. After family party he ended up in the emergency room and had his stomach pumped. A day later it was discovered the distention of his stomach had caused a loss of blood flow. The stomach became septic and ruptured. He died from complications.

His father stated in the article people with the syndrome are good at what they do, accessing extra food, it can happen quickly.

This story taught me four things, the futility of worry, the importance of vigilance, the necessity of keeping people with the syndrome safe, and how the syndrome mirrors addiction. I spent so much time worrying about Robert's weight, and the consequences of morbid obesity. Now it is a non-issue, he weighs about 158. Other aspects of the syndrome are much more worrisome, if I would allow myself to go there.

I mention addiction again because more people are educated about sobriety and relapse. An AA anecdote tells of a recovered person attending a meeting while their addiction does pushups in the parking lot. PWS syndrome mimics an addict accessing what they crave and paying with their life.

Denise's Story

Denise is a speech pathologist and the mother of three. Her middle daughter Maya, has Prader-Willi. Her oldest is Maddie, 14, and the youngest is Mallory, 7. I mention this because when I heard her story I thought how brave she was to have another child after giving birth to a special needs child. It is a secret thought most of us have. Maya is a classic example, the onset of behaviors occurred at age 5. The challenges she presented sent Denise to a behaviorist, who helped find ways to cope with behaviors.

The family uses rewards instead of consequences, which prove ineffective. Denise also followed her behaviorist's advice and let Maya do the things she would argue she wanted to do. While shoe shopping at Target Maya wanted to try on toddler shoes. Denise initially said "Those are too small they won't fit." Maya disagreed, once she was allowed to try them on, she saw for herself they were too small. "You were right Mom; these are too small," Maya said. One point for Mom!

Denise is also unusual in the sense she is not afraid of placing Maya in a group home. She has seen several of them during her working hours and knows the structure of a group home will decrease her daughter's anxiety about food. Most of the parents of younger children with PWS fear placement, like I did.

When I met with Denise we discussed her connection with Roxann Diez Gross, a PhD in speech pathology at the Children's Institute of Pittsburgh. Denise had heard her speak after graduating from the University of Virginia. Dr. Gross specializes in the swallowing function. She is doing a swallowing study of people with PWS. Patients often have food in their esophagus which they are not aware of and choke easily on food. Initially, the hospital removed foods from the diet patients choked on. Now, with the study completed Dr. Gross recommends serving water with meals, to move food down the esophagus. The Institute has been successful in implementing this plan.

Kristy's Story

Kristy Rickenbach travels long distances with her twelve-year-old daughter Justice to see an Endocrinologist. She treats Justice for disorders in her gastrointestinal system, a problem common in PWS. Kristi says, her doctor assures me I have a beautiful daughter and helps me not to feel alone." She is committed to finding the best doctors available to treat her child. Many of the parents I spoke to are equally passionate in seeking out knowledgeable physicians.

Kristy and I have both visited South Africa. Each of us had a mind-bending experience there. Many people in South Africa believe having a special needs child is a punishment for doing something bad. These babies are often abandoned.

On a tour of one of the Townships in Cape Town with a mission group from my church, we saw a place where special needs children were housed. One young girl greeted our group when we arrived. She was washing clothes in a large plastic bucket. Can you imagine doing your family's wash this way? The children spent most of their day lying on sheets placed over the dirt floor. Two women watched over multiple babies, with the assistance of older children.

Kristi's experience was very like my own. She saw similar hopeless situations in her travels across Africa. She said "The conditions these children live in are horrible, I can still remember the way it smelled"

Both of us wanted to help, our hearts broke for these children. I thought maybe some information on how to care for and stimulate these babies would help. When I got home I contacted Pacer. They educate and advocate for people with disabilities. Pacer has many pamphlets which offer fantastic information on how to advocate for your child. None of them seemed appropriate. Much of the information centered around navigating the school system. Important for people who have access to schools, these children would never attend school. I pray for them often.

Kristi and her husband have a more concrete approach. They offer a Bible-based archery program called Center Shot to school children in both the USA and Africa.

Learning a skill such as this gives people a sense of accomplishment.

I write about the children of Africa because often we feel overwhelmed without problems. At least help is available in this country to people determined to access it. You can network with friends, teachers, family, coworkers, church ministry and members. Someone will know where to access what you need. Be relentless, you may not find what you need on the first try, eventually, you will find it.

Balance is a current buzz word in our culture. Don't let it become one more unattainable goal. When I speak to others who are self-employed we all agree. It is either feast or famine. The hard times will make you more appreciative when things are easier. Take advantage of your less busy times to recharge, don't agonize about not having something to do. Make some friends who you can laugh with and who can cheer you up. Do things to make yourself happy. Taking some time for you is not selfish— it is good self-care. You will enjoy life more, and the people in your life will enjoy you!

Carey and I are now empty nesters. He continues to enjoy work while I collect Social Security. Carey gets many vacation days that are generally used traveling to see family. Cath David their daughter Kelly and family all moved to Hawaii. We miss the frequent contact we once had and stay in close touch. Vacations in tropical islands are a great escape from our cold Minnesota winter. Their son Steve continues to live here and share time with us at the family cabin in the summer.

Cara along with husband Justin and twelve- year old son Rory live twenty minutes away. We see each other often, going to Rory's sporting events, movies, and coffee time. Cara has her RN degree in nursing, and works at Regions in cardiac care. She is compassionate caring and very competent. The friendship and love she shares with her Dad is beautiful to see. They both have a love of technology, and have the same sense of humor. Our relationship has continued to improve over the years. I am so proud of all she has accomplished. We are still two completely different people. I try to listen more without giving advice. I follow my Mom's example of being available to help with Rory on short notice. Who doesn't love time with their Grandson? Rory states "everyone should have a superpower, Robert's is manipulation." He understands his Uncle and share an enjoyment of video games. Cara realizes she will one day be responsible for her brother's care. I'm sure it's not something she looks forward to. It is something she will do well.

The life Robert leads now is a busy one. He earns most of his rewards on a regular basis. He gets a Dairy Queen Blizzard every Wednesday and a meal out on Saturday. He participates in Special Olympics swimming, softball, track, and poly hockey. Courage Center offers a ski program twenty minutes from Hastings at Welsh Village. I recently joined him for a morning of skiing with the volunteers. He now skis between two volunteers holding a bamboo pole.

They blast down the hill, completing several turns, leaving Mom behind. It is truly astounding! Robert goes with us to our lake cabin in the summer and he usually has a week at Courage Horse Camp, too. He rides Dakota, the horse I lease, and can ride at a trot independently. Robert told me, "Dakota is my spirit animal. He is always trying to get at the hay bales in the arena."

Writing this book brought back many memories. As a child and even a young adult I let circumstances control me. I felt powerless and just wanted the pain to go away. I used drugs alcohol and food to medicate. Certainly I never saw the life I have now coming! I believe I survived Addiction, Cancer, and Robert's traumatic birth for a reason. I am passionate about improving my son's life and the life of others with PWS. Sharing intimate details of your family's struggles are risky, you open yourself to criticism, especially in today's culture. I wanted to give an honest account of the emotions, both positive and negative, our family experienced. While medical care improves, families who have a child with PWS are still coping with an unknown outcome.

The people I met though my church, work, friendships, and the organizations we worked with were life changing. Of course, you can meet great people even if your child doesn't have a life threatening syndrome. Yet, I don't think my heart would have been as open to receive everything I was given, and appreciate it. I live, what I refer to as "my very fun life."

I spend part of each day outside, either gardening, swimming, horseback riding, or walking our dog. It keeps me grounded and calm. I've volunteered for many organizations giving back a little bit. Traveling has enriched my view of the world and fulfilled the dreams of seeing the world I had as a child. I have learned to accept things the way they are, but it's a daily struggle. I choose to be happy every day.

For the families who may be just beginning this journey, remember, the only time any of us have is now. Worrying about future problems will steal today's joy. None of the things I obsessed about ever happened. When something did go wrong, we found a way through it. My hope is other families will find our story will help them in some way. The fear we experienced as young parents hindered our ability to live in the "now." I encourage you to find the help you need so you can enjoy your life.

ROBERT RORY AND CAREY AT A RUN CLUB
BANQUET VERBAL CORRECTIONS

ACKNOWLEDGEMENTS

I would like to thank my husband Carey for being such a great life partner who never lets me take myself too seriously. Thank you to my writer friend Carol Pine. She told me "you are a good story teller." It made me want to be one. So many people helped me along the way. My sister Cath read the first draft and said "This is good." Thank you to my daughter Cara who allowed me to share her life, as well as the others mentioned in this book who let me tell their stories.

Thank you to niece Kelly who did a first edit, it wasn't pretty! Bonnie Bates inspired me with her passionate advocacy for people with the syndrome. I also want to thank Diane Keyes and Gloria VanDemmeltraadt for editing, along with the Woman of Words writing group. They made it a much better book. Ann Aubitz from FuzionPrint took me though publishing. Thank you Rahi Riazi with Copperblu Media for book promotion A big thank you to Robert, who was not crazy about being in a book!

OUR FAMILY

RESOURCES

Allina Health
Courage Kenny Sports and Rec W
3915 Golden Valley Road Mpls. MN. 55422
763-588-0811

Office for the Ombudsman for Mental Health and Developmental Disabilities (State of Minnesota)
www.ombudsman.mhdd@state.mn.us
121th Place E., Suite 420
Metro Square Building
St. Paul MN 55101-2117
651-729-1950

NAMI
National Alliance on Mental Health
800 Transfer RD #3
St Paul MN. 55114
651-645-2948 toll free 1-888-626-4435
namihelps@namimn.org

Majestic Hills Ranch
24580 Dakota Ave.
Lakeville MN. 55044
Children's program 952-426-5688
Hero's on Horseback riding for injured veterans
612-669-8846
majestichillsranch.org

Pacer Center
8161 Normandale Blvd. Mpls. Mn.55437
952-838-9000 Pacer.org

Prader-Willi Syndrome Association USA National Office
8588 Potter Park Drive Suite 500 Sarasota FL. 34238
800-926-4797   WWW.pwsausa.org
Prader-Willi Syndrome Association Minnesota Chapter
Kristi Richenbach President
763-242-9074   Kristi-cole@yahoo.com

People Incorporated
2060 Centre Pointe Blvd. Suite 3
St Paul MN. 55120
651-774-0011 peopleincorporated.org

We can Ride
14300 Co Rd. 42 Minnetonka MN.
952-934-0057
wecanride.org

www.ingramcontent.com/pod-product-compliance
Lightning Source LLC
LaVergne TN
LVHW011352080426
835511LV00005B/258